green
vegetarian food

Published by Murdoch Books®, a division of Murdoch Magazines Pty Ltd.

Murdoch Books® Australia
Pier 8/9, 23 Hickson Road
Miller's Point NSW 2000
Phone: +61 (0) 2 4352 7000
Fax: +61 (0) 2 4352 7026

Murdoch Books UK Limited
Erico House
6th Floor North
93–99 Upper Richmond Road
Putney, London SW15 2TG
Phone: +44 (0) 20 8785 5995
Fax: +44 (0) 20 8785 5985

Design Concept: Marylouise Brammer
Designer: Tracy Louglin
Editorial Director: Diana Hill
Additional Text: Francesca Newby
Project Manager: Zoë Harpham
Editor: Katri Hilden
Consultant Food Editor: Jane Lawson
Production: Monika Vidovic
Recipes developed and tested by the Murdoch Books Test Kitchen.

Chief Executive: Juliet Rogers
Publisher: Kay Scarlett

National Library of Australia Cataloguing-in-Publication Data
Green. Includes index. ISBN 1 74045 264 X
1. Vegetarian cookery. 641.5636

PRINTED IN CHINA by Toppan Printing Co. (HK) Ltd.
Printed 2004.

IMPORTANT: Those who might be at risk from the effects of salmonella food poisoning (the elderly, pregnant
women, young children and those suffering from immune deficiency diseases) should consult their doctor with
any concerns about eating raw eggs.

green
vegetarian food

MURDOCH BOOKS

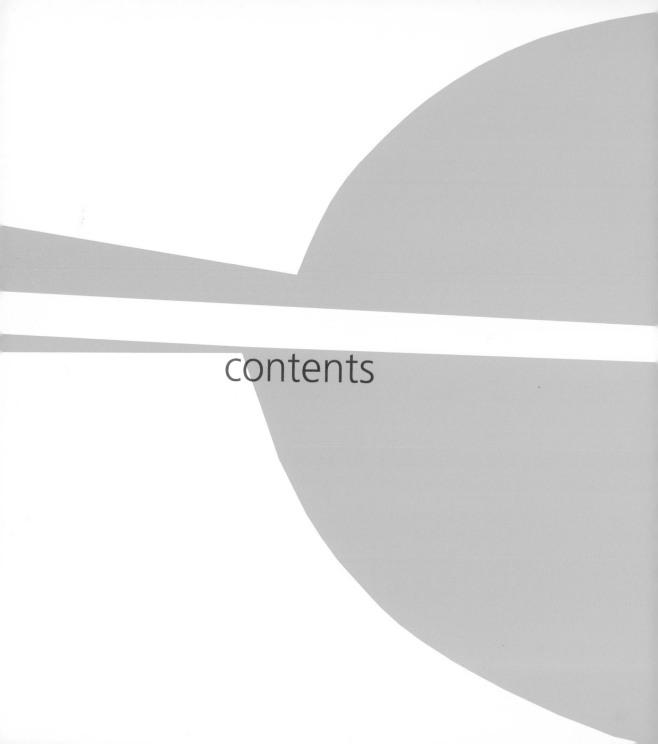

contents

green is good

here's to your health!

In the flow of information about healthy eating, good nutrition and broader environmental concerns, there is one facet of vegetarian food that tends to slip beneath the radar: the fact that it is simply delicious. Forget the outdated image of vegetarian food as worthy and boring — with the abundance of market-fresh ingredients available today, there are really no excuses for dull, monotonous meals.

Refreshing, succulent, hearty or light, there is a meal in this book to satisfy every taste and every desire. Whether you are planning a rowdy get-together or a lingering breakfast for two, dinner with the in-laws or a late supper in front of the telly, think outside the square and reach into the vegetable crisper. From the homely to the exotic, the recipes in this book are drawn from all corners of the globe, with a few modern classics thrown in for good measure.

This is food to nourish the soul as well as the body, so think 'green' and go organic or biodynamic wherever you can. Whatever your reasons for being a vegetarian, with these wonderful recipes at hand you'll remember why you made such a natural, healthy choice. How fabulous when your food doesn't just make you feel good, but also does you good!

rise and shine

delectable ways to start your day

This marvellous dish really is worth getting out of bed for — but unless you're planning a seriously late breakfast, marinate the haloumi the night before. Then, once you've tumbled out of bed, you can fry it all up in the blink of a bleary eye.

fried green tomatoes with haloumi

2 garlic cloves, crushed
2 tbs lemon juice
1 tbs balsamic vinegar
3 tbs extra virgin olive oil
500 g (1 lb 2 oz) haloumi cheese, cut into
1 cm (1/2 inch) thick slices
250 g (1 punnet) cherry tomatoes
250 g (1 punnet) teardrop tomatoes, halved
4 green tomatoes, thickly sliced
125 ml (1/2 cup) buttermilk
150 g (1 cup) polenta (cornmeal)
oil, for shallow-frying
100 g (1 bunch) rocket (arugula)
2 tsp marjoram

First to the haloumi. In a non-metallic dish, mix together the garlic, lemon juice, balsamic vinegar and olive oil, then add the slices of haloumi. Leave to marinate for at least 3 hours, or overnight if possible.

When you're ready to eat, lift the haloumi out of the dish, but keep the lovely marinade. Fry the haloumi in a non-stick frying pan over medium heat until deliciously golden on both sides, about 1–2 minutes each side. Remove from the pan and set aside.

Now fry all the tiny tomatoes for 3–4 minutes until the skins burst, then take them out of the pan and keep them warm. Pour the marinade into the pan, heat it through, then add it to the cooked tomatoes.

Now to the green tomatoes — first dip them into the buttermilk, then coat them in the polenta. Heat some oil in a large, non-stick frying pan and fry the tomatoes over medium heat until brown, about 2 minutes each side. Drain on paper towels.

Put a bed of rocket on four serving plates. Arrange the haloumi slices on top, with the fried green tomatoes and the tiny tomatoes. Drizzle with the marinade, sprinkle with marjoram and enjoy without delay.
Serves 4.

poached eggs with yoghurt dressing and spinach

125 g (1/2 cup) sheep's yoghurt
1 small garlic clove, crushed
1 tbs snipped chives
300 g (10 1/2 oz) baby English spinach
30 g (1 1/2 tbs) butter, chopped
herbed salt, or good sea salt
4 tomatoes, halved
1 tbs white vinegar
8 very fresh free-range eggs
8 slices of rye bread, toasted

Make a piquant dressing for the eggs by mixing together the yoghurt, garlic and chives. Keep it away from roaming fingers until you're ready to serve.

Wash the spinach and put it in a large saucepan with a little water clinging to the leaves. Pop the lid on and cook over low heat for a few minutes, until the leaves wilt. Add the butter and gently stir until it melts and the leaves are glistening. Season with some herbed salt, and keep somewhere warm.

Cook the tomatoes under a hot grill (broiler) for a few minutes and keep them warm.

Now onto the eggs. Fill a large frying pan three-quarters full with cold water and splash in the vinegar and some salt. Bring the water to a gentle simmer. Gently break an egg into a small bowl and carefully slide it into the water. Do the same with the other eggs, then reduce the heat so that the water in the pan barely moves. Cook for 1–2 minutes, or until the eggs are just set. Lift them out of the pan with a spatula or slotted spoon, draining well.

Top each slice of toast with the spinach, a poached egg and some yoghurt dressing, and serve with the warm tomato halves. Serves 4.

Soft poached eggs dressed in piquant fresh yoghurt: such an easy way to slide into the day. A touch of garlic can be enjoyed for breakfast — just make sure you've had all your morning kisses first!

So very health giving, this nutty, fruity muesli is perfect for the morning after the night before. Graze on a big bowl of it and you'll be feeling virtuous when you finally waltz out the door.

healthy nut and seed muesli

100 g (3¹/₂ oz) puffed corn
150 g (1¹/₂ cups) rolled oats
100 g (1 cup) pecans
160 g (1 cup) macadamias, roughly chopped
110 g (2 cups) flaked coconut
200 g (7 oz) LSA (linseed, sunflower and almond mix)
115 g (1¹/₄ cups) chopped dried apples
185 g (1 cup) chopped dried apricots
125 g (4¹/₂ oz) dried pears, chopped
125 ml (¹/₂ cup) maple syrup
1 tsp natural vanilla extract

Get a large bowl and tip in all the grains, nuts and fruit and roughly mix together.

Pour the maple syrup and vanilla into a small saucepan. Gently heat it just enough so that the maple syrup becomes easy to pour — a few minutes should do. Once the mixture is at pouring consistency, drizzle it over the dry ingredients, then mix it all through so everything is sticky with syrup.

Divide the muesli mixture between two non-stick baking trays. Bake in a 180°C (350°F/Gas 4) oven until the muesli is lightly toasted, 20 minutes or so, stirring frequently so it is evenly toasted. Let the muesli cool completely, then stash it in an airtight container.
Makes 1 kg (2 lb 4 oz).

tex mex cornbread with scrambled eggs

For the cornbread:
155 g (1½ cups) self-raising flour
1 tbs caster (superfine) sugar
2 tsp baking powder
110 g (¾ cup) fine polenta (cornmeal)
60 g (½ cup) grated Cheddar cheese
15 g (½ cup) chopped coriander
(cilantro) leaves
2 teaspoons ground cumin
large pinch of cayenne pepper
2 fresh free-range eggs
250 ml (1 cup) buttermilk
4 tbs corn oil

For the scrambled eggs:
6 fresh free-range eggs
125 ml (½ cup) cream
coriander (cilantro) leaves

To make the cornbread, sift the flour, sugar, baking powder and 1 teaspoon salt into a bowl. Add the polenta, cheese, coriander, cumin, cayenne pepper, eggs, buttermilk and oil and mix thoroughly. Spoon the mixture into a 20 x 10 cm (8 x 4 inch) loaf tin and bake in a 180°C (350°F/Gas 4) oven until a skewer comes out clean, about 45 minutes. Remove the cornbread from the tin.

To make the scrambled eggs, whisk together the eggs and cream and season with salt and pepper. Pour the mixture into a non-stick frying pan and cook over low heat, stirring occasionally, until the egg is just set — if you can resist stirring too much, you'll be rewarded with smooth, creamy eggs. Serve the scrambled eggs with generously buttered cornbread, sprinkled with a few coriander leaves.
Serves 4.

Discover the joy of baking bread while all and sundry slumber on around you, then eat it all yourself before they wake up — why save any for the lazy bones?

These tarts are an excellent hangover remedy when you're feeling decidedly seedy. In the sober light of morning, they will help restock your body with all the vitamins you've thrashed out of it. Of course, you don't need a fuzzy head to utterly enjoy them.

chunky ratatouille tarts

1 eggplant (aubergine), cut into generous cubes
1 red capsicum (pepper), cut into biggish squares
3 zucchini (courgettes), thickly sliced
1 red onion, cut into large pieces
2 tbs olive oil
200 g (7 oz) teardrop or cherry tomatoes
140 g (3/4 cup) Kalamata olives, pitted
2 tbs finely shredded basil, plus a little extra
2 sheets frozen puff pastry, thawed
1 free-range egg, lightly beaten

Throw the eggplant cubes into a roasting tin with the capsicum, zucchini and onion. Drizzle with the oil and toss well, then bake in a 200°C (400°F/Gas 6) oven for 40 minutes, tossing frequently. Now add the tomatoes and bake for another 5 minutes.

Scoop all the vegetables into a bowl, stir in the olives and basil, and season with salt and pepper. Strain the mixture well.

Cut one pastry sheet into four squares and lay them on a baking tray lined with baking paper. Cut the second sheet in half, then cut sixteen 2 cm (3/4 inch) wide pastry strips to fit around the edges of each square. Divide the ratatouille among the squares, brush the pastry edges with beaten egg and bake until the tarts are golden, about 25 minutes. Sprinkle with a little basil and enjoy while nice and hot.
Serves 4.

cinnamon porridge with grilled figs

200 g (2 cups) rolled oats
1/4 tsp ground cinnamon
50 g (1³/4 oz) butter
95 g (1/2 cup) soft brown sugar
300 ml (10¹/2 fl oz) cream
6 fresh figs, halved
large pinch of ground ginger
milk, for serving

First, make the porridge. Put the oats, cinnamon and 1 litre (4 cups) water in a saucepan and stir over medium heat until you have a thick, hot, smooth porridge — about 5 minutes. Take the pan off the hob, and keep warm while you're preparing the rest of the breakfast.

Melt the butter in a large frying pan and when it's sizzling, add all but 2 tablespoons of the brown sugar and give it a good stir until it dissolves into a gorgeous caramel butter. Stir in the cream and bring to the boil, then simmer until the sauce starts to thicken slightly — 5 minutes should do.

Lay the figs on a baking tray with the cut sides facing up. Now combine the remaining sugar with the ground ginger and sprinkle it over the figs. Grill (broil) until the sugar has melted and the figs have softened.

Spoon the porridge into four bowls, pour on a little milk, then divide the figs and caramel sauce among the bowls. Hmmmm …
Serves 4.

Sensuous figs, their flowers coyly hidden on the inside, were a favourite with Cleopatra. Try scattering them on this creamy, aromatic porridge and share it with your Antony.

Light, fluffy flatcakes flecked with coconut, lemon and ricotta make an admirable start to the morning. Banana gives you extra bounce, and palm sugar a sprinkling of the exotic.

coconut and ricotta flatcakes with banana

150 g (1 cup) wholemeal flour
2 tsp baking powder
2 tbs caster (superfine) sugar
55 g (1 cup) flaked coconut, lightly toasted
1 tsp finely grated lemon zest
4 free-range eggs, separated
340 g (1^1/$_3$ cups) ricotta cheese
310 ml (1^1/$_4$ cups) milk
4 bananas, sliced
coconut cream
2 tbs shaved palm sugar

Sift the flour, baking powder and sugar into a large bowl. Stir in the coconut and lemon zest and make a well in the centre. In a separate bowl, combine the egg yolks, ricotta and milk, then stir into the flour mixture until you have a smooth batter.

Now beat the egg whites until soft, billowy peaks form, then gently fold them into the batter — the egg whites help the flatcakes become light and fluffy.

Heat a frying pan and brush lightly with a little melted butter or oil. Pour ^{1}/$_4$ cup (about 3 tablespoons) of the batter into the pan and swirl gently to create an even flatcake. Cook over low heat until bubbles form on the surface, then flip the flatcake over and cook the other side for a minute until golden. To keep your flatcakes warm, stack them on a plate, covered with a foil tent, in a moderate oven while you cook the rest.

Stack three warm flatcakes onto each plate and top with some sliced banana. Drizzle with a little coconut cream, top with some shaved palm sugar and tuck in at once. Serves 4.

crispy lavash tiles with buttered mushrooms

3 pieces of lavash or pitta bread
2 tbs olive oil
3 tbs finely grated Parmesan cheese
750 g (1 lb 10 oz) mixed mushrooms
(we used field, button, Swiss browns,
shimeji and enoki)
100 g (3¹/2 oz) butter
4 spring onions (scallions), sliced
1 tbs chopped chervil

Cut the bread into 3 cm (1¹/4 inch) wide strips and brush lightly with 1 tablespoon of the oil. Sprinkle with the grated Parmesan and bake in a 180°C (350°F/Gas 4) oven until crispy, about 10 minutes.

Meanwhile, slice all the mushrooms except the shimeji and enoki, which just need to have their ends trimmed before being gently separated. Heat the butter and remaining oil in a large frying pan and, when sizzling, add the spring onions and field, button and Swiss brown mushrooms and fry over medium heat until the mushrooms are tender, about 8–10 minutes.

Now add the shimeji mushrooms and cook until the liquid has evaporated, about 4 minutes. Remove the pan from the heat and stir through the enoki mushrooms — they're so tender that the heat still in the pan will cook them enough.

Arrange the toasted strips of lavash bread into an interlocking square, using at least four strips of lavash per serve. Pile the mushrooms in the centre, sprinkle with chervil and start munching.
Serves 4.

Mushrooms aren't just delicious, they are very, very good for you — so pile your plate high and congratulate yourself on your clever choice of breakfast.

Hot, light and crispy, these waffles should be made in bulk and consumed instantly. If you don't have a waffle iron, run out and buy one immediately!

cheese and onion waffles with herbed ricotta and roast tomato

For the roasted tomatoes:
4 Roma (plum) tomatoes, cut in half
1 tbs olive oil
1 tbs balsamic vinegar
1 tsp sugar
1 tbs chopped oregano

For the ricotta dumplings:
310 g (1¼ cups) low-fat ricotta cheese
4 tbs chopped herbs (such as oregano, sage, rosemary, parsley)

For the waffles:
185 g (1½ cups) self-raising flour
3 tbs freshly grated Parmesan cheese
3 tbs grated low-fat Cheddar cheese
3 large spring onions (scallions), finely chopped
1 free-range egg
250 ml (1 cup) low-fat milk
2 free-range egg whites

Firstly, roast the tomato halves. Put them on a lightly greased baking tray, cut sides facing up. Lightly drizzle with olive oil and balsamic vinegar, then sprinkle with the sugar, oregano and a little salt. Bake in a 160°C (315°F/Gas 2–3) oven for an hour so the tomatoes become very soft.

Meanwhile, make the ricotta dumplings. Plop the ricotta into a bowl and fold in the chopped herbs. Season to taste. Using two tablespoons, shape the mixture into 8 round or oval dumplings. Keep them in the fridge until you need them.

To make the waffle batter, put the flour, Parmesan, Cheddar, spring onion, whole egg and milk in a bowl. Season with salt and black pepper, then mix well. Whisk the egg whites until soft peaks form, and gently fold into the waffle mixture.

Heat a waffle iron and brush lightly with olive oil. Pour in ⅓ cup (about 4 tablespoons) of the waffle batter and cook until golden on both sides. Keep warm in the oven while you cook the remaining waffles.

To serve, arrange two waffle halves on each serving plate with two tomato halves and two fresh ricotta dumplings on the side. Devour while hot.
Serves 4.

scrambled tofu with mushrooms

2 tbs butter
200 g (7 oz) button mushrooms, sliced
1 garlic clove, crushed
2 spring onions (scallions), chopped
400 g (14 oz) firm tofu, drained and crumbled
1 tsp tamari
1 tbs finely chopped parsley
8 thick slices of your favourite bread, toasted

Melt 1 tablespoon of the butter in a large frying pan. Throw in the mushrooms and cook over high heat for 5 minutes, or until they start to lose their moisture. Now add the garlic and cook for a further 5 minutes, or until the liquid has evaporated. Take the mushrooms out for a moment.

Now melt the remaining butter in the pan, add the spring onion and briefly cook until just wilted. Throw the mushrooms back in with the tofu and tamari and cook, stirring gently, until the tofu is heated through — about 2 minutes. Stir in the parsley, season generously with black pepper, and serve hot on buttered toast.
Serves 4.

Firm, medium, soft and silky are bedroom terms to some, but grades of tofu to those in the know. When you're turning up the heat, go for firm tofu to stop it disintegrating in the pan.

This is five-star French toast made in the Italian way, with a quick detour east. Definitely one to remember when you've got something to celebrate — a wedding, an anniversary or just having made it out of bed.

pandoro with poached peaches and mascarpone

220 g (1 cup) sugar
3 cardamom pods, bruised
1 bay leaf
1 vanilla bean, split
juice of 1 lemon
6 peaches
500 ml (2 cups) milk
2 free-range eggs, lightly beaten
4 small pandoro (a rich yellow
Italian yeast cake), thickly sliced,
or 1 small panettone, sliced
50 g (2¹/2 tbs) butter
165 g (³/4 cup) mascarpone cheese
3 tbs soft brown sugar

Start by making a fragrant poaching syrup. Put the sugar, cardamom pods, bay leaf, vanilla bean and lemon juice in a large saucepan with 1 litre (4 cups) water. Stir over low heat until the sugar dissolves. Now bring to the boil and add the peaches. Reduce the heat and simmer for 10 minutes. Lift the peaches out of the syrup, then neatly peel and halve them. To thicken the syrup, boil it until reduced by a third.

Mix the milk and eggs together in a shallow bowl, then dip the pandoro slices into the mixture and give them a good, even coating.

Now melt the butter in a frying pan. When it sizzles, add the pandoro and fry over medium heat until golden on both sides, about 2–3 minutes each side.

Meanwhile, make yourself a decadent accompaniment by mixing together the mascarpone and brown sugar.

Arrange the warm pandoro slices on four plates, top with a dollop of mascarpone and three peach halves, and drizzle with some of the poaching syrup. Heaven. Serves 4.

mixed berry couscous

185 g (1 cup) couscous
500 ml (2 cups) apple and cranberry juice
1 cinnamon stick
125 g (1/2 punnet) raspberries
125 g (1/2 punnet) blueberries
125 g (1/2 punnet) blackberries
125 g (1/2 punnet) strawberries, halved
zest of 1 lime
zest of 1 orange
250 g (1 cup) thick Greek-style yoghurt
2 tbs golden syrup

This recipe is so simple! First, pour the couscous into a large bowl.

Now pour the apple and cranberry juice into a saucepan with the cinnamon stick. Bring to the boil, then remove from the heat and pour the mixture over the couscous, cinnamon stick and all. Cover with plastic wrap and let the liquid absorb into the couscous — this will take about 5 minutes. Now you can take out the cinnamon stick.

Fluff the couscous with a fork, then add all the berries and citrus zest and fold gently through the couscous. Spoon into four bowls and serve with a generous dollop of yoghurt and a drizzling of golden syrup.
Serves 4.

Sunshine in a bowl, this beautiful summer brekky deserves to be eaten lounging about outside, watching the clouds drift by.

Get your motor running on a drab winter morning with a steaming bowl of porridge. Lashings of tangy rhubarb chase away the blues.

home-made porridge with stewed rhubarb

For the porridge:
600 g (6 cups) rolled oats
55 g (1/2 cup) rolled rice flakes
60 g (1/2 cup) rolled barley
60 g (1/2 cup) rolled rye
3 tbs millet flakes

For the stewed rhubarb:
350 g (12 oz) rhubarb, chopped into short lengths
95 g (1/2 cup) soft brown sugar
1/4 tsp ground mixed spice

Combine all the porridge ingredients and store in a large airtight jar until ready to use.

To make porridge for four, put one-quarter of the dry mixture (about 2 cups) in a saucepan with 1.25 litres (5 cups) water. Bring to the boil, then reduce the heat and simmer over medium heat for 15 minutes, stirring frequently so you have a smooth, lump-free porridge. Check the consistency — you might like to add a little skim milk if the porridge is too thick for you.

Meanwhile, make the stewed rhubarb. Put the rhubarb in a saucepan with the sugar, mixed spice and 250 ml (1 cup) water. Slowly bring to the boil, stirring to dissolve the sugar, then reduce the heat and simmer for about 10 minutes, stirring often. Enjoy hot or cold with the porridge.
Serves 4.

individual herbed baked lemon ricotta

500 g (2 cups) ricotta cheese
crusty bread, to serve

For the lemon dressing:
2 tbs olive oil
1 garlic clove, crushed
zest of 1 lemon
2 tbs lemon juice
1 tbs balsamic vinegar
125 ml (1/2 cup) olive oil
150 g (51/2 oz) semi-dried (sun-blushed)
tomatoes, roughly chopped
4 tbs chopped parsley

Lightly grease and then line four 125 ml (1/2 cup) ramekins with plastic wrap. Divide the ricotta among the moulds and press down firmly. Cover with plastic wrap and refrigerate for 2 hours.

Unmould the ricotta mounds onto a baking tray lined with baking paper, then bake in a 220°C (425°F/Gas 7) oven until golden, about 20 minutes or so.

Meanwhile, make the lemon dressing: simply combine all the ingredients in a small bowl.

Divide the baked ricotta rounds among four shallow serving bowls. Spoon a little lemon dressing over each one, and serve straight away with crusty bread.
Serves 4.

Perfect for a crisp winter morning, these golden mounds of goodness will warm you up without weighing you down. A zing of lemon lifts the creamy ricotta into the realms of the sublime.

When it's way too hot for a cooked breakfast, reach into the freezer and pull out some icy granita, which you very sensibly made in the cool of the evening before. For extra tingle, serve it up with your favourite fruit — some lush mango cheeks, perhaps?

tangy mandarin lime granita

230 g (1 cup) caster (superfine) sugar
1 tsp finely chopped mandarin zest
1 tsp finely chopped lime zest
500 ml (2 cups) mandarin juice

Put the sugar in a saucepan with 125 ml (1/2 cup) water and stir over a low heat until the sugar dissolves. Bring to the boil and cook over high heat until the mixture becomes syrupy, about 5 minutes.

Take the pan off the hob, then stir in all the zest and the mandarin juice. Pour into a shallow metal tray, cover with foil and place in the freezer for 1 hour, or until the edges begin to freeze. Scrape with a fork to break up the ice crystals, then cover and return to the freezer.

Repeat four times at 50-minute intervals, then allow the granita to freeze completely. When you're ready to rumble, use a fork to scrape the granita into large shavings, and serve at once in small bowls.
Serves 4.

maple yoghurt balls with sugary balsamic pears

1 kg (4 cups) thick Greek-style yoghurt
125 ml (1/2 cup) maple syrup
1 tbs ground cinnamon
2 tbs caster (superfine) sugar
180 g (1 1/2 cups) hazelnuts, toasted
and roughly chopped
150 g (5 1/2 oz) butter
95 g (1/2 cup) soft brown sugar
3 tbs balsamic vinegar
3 small beurre bosc pears, sliced lengthways

Though the yoghurt balls are very easy to make, they do need to be started four days ahead. So let's get started!

Mix together the yoghurt and maple syrup, scoop onto a large square of doubled muslin, gather the muslin together and tie up tightly with string. Loop the string around a chopstick and suspend over a bowl in the fridge for four days to drain off any liquid.

When you're ready to roll, mix the cinnamon and sugar together in a bowl. Using moistened hands, roll 1 tablespoon of the drained yoghurt mixture into a ball. Roll it around in the cinnamon sugar, then gently toss to coat in the chopped hazelnuts. Repeat with the remaining mixture.

Heat the butter in a large frying pan, add the brown sugar and stir over low heat until it dissolves. Now stir in the vinegar and bring the mixture to the boil. Add the pears and simmer until browned on both sides and slightly soft, about 1–2 minutes each side. Arrange on serving plates, top with the yoghurt balls, then savour every mouthful. Serves 4.

Perfect for a celebration, these creamy marvels need plenty of planning. Make them for Easter Sunday, a naming ceremony, a wedding breakfast or the summer solstice – any day that matters to you.

Highly prized as an aphrodisiac, vanilla beans were once the preserve of royalty. As seductive as ever, their tiny seeds add a smooth, velvety undertone to this spicy summer salad.

star anise, lime and vanilla tropical fruit salad

1 kg (2 lb 4 oz) watermelon, cut into chunks
1 small pineapple, peeled and chopped
2 mangoes, sliced
1 guava, sliced
1 small red papaya, cut into chunks
12 lychees, peeled
3 kiwifruit, sliced

For the syrup:
3 tbs lime juice
135 g (3/4 cup) grated light palm sugar
6 star anise seeds
1 vanilla bean, split
1 pandanus leaf, knotted
zest of 1 lime

Put all the fruit in a bowl and gently combine into a colourful, vibrant salad.

Now make the syrup, the secret to this zesty salad. Simply put all the ingredients into a saucepan with 250 ml (1 cup) water and stir over low heat until the sugar dissolves. Bring to the boil, reduce the heat and simmer until reduced by half, about 10 minutes. Allow to cool slightly, then pour the syrup over the fruit and refrigerate until cold. Serves 6.

pancakes with rosewater strawberries and butter

185 g (1¹/₂ cups) self-raising flour
1 tsp baking powder
2 tbs caster (superfine) sugar
2 free-range eggs, lightly beaten
250 ml (1 cup) milk
60 g (2¹/₄ oz) butter, melted,
plus a little extra
100 g (3¹/₂ oz) unsalted butter,
softened and whipped

For the rosewater strawberries:
400 g (14 oz) strawberries, halved
2 tsp rosewater
1 tsp natural vanilla extract
3 tbs maple syrup

Start with the pancake batter. Sift the flour, baking powder, sugar and a pinch of salt into a bowl and make a well in the centre. In a jug, mix together the eggs, milk and melted butter and pour into the well. Whisk to form a smooth batter, then cover and let stand for 20 minutes.

Meanwhile, make the rosewater strawberries: all you need to do is mix all the ingredients together in a bowl.

Once the pancake batter has rested, heat a non-stick frying pan and brush with a little extra melted butter. Pour ¹/₄ cup (about 3 tablespoons) of batter into the pan and swirl gently. Cook over low heat until bubbles burst on the surface, about 1 minute. Flip the pancake over and cook the other side. Don't worry if the first one is a bit of a flop, the rest will be perfect. Transfer to a plate and keep warm while you cook the other pancakes.

Serve the pancakes in stacks, topped with whipped butter and those delicious rosewater strawberries.
Serves 4.

When the morning calls for romance, as all good mornings should, serve a stack of these exquisite pancakes with flutes of crisp golden Champagne infused with a drop of rosewater.

Sophisticated cousins of cinnamon toast, these scrumptious crumpet fingers are creamy, spicy and light all at once. A fruit compote makes them extra special — in summer, try one made from berries or stonefruit.

fruit compote with cinnamon crumpet fingers

For the fruit compote:
200 g (7 oz) pitted prunes
200 g (7 oz) fresh dates, pitted and halved
400 g (14 oz) dried fruit salad mix
500 ml (2 cups) apple juice

For the cinnamon sugar:
1 tbs ground cinnamon
3 tbs sugar

4 crumpets
20 g (1 tbs) butter
200 g (7 oz) low-fat vanilla fromage frais
or whipped yoghurt

First, start with the fruit compote. Put the prunes, dates and dried fruits in a saucepan with the apple juice. Bring to the boil, then reduce the heat and simmer for 15 minutes, or until the fruit is plump and tender.

Meanwhile, mix together the cinnamon sugar ingredients in a small bowl.

Toast the crumpets until golden brown, then spread lightly with butter. Sprinkle with the cinnamon sugar, then cut the crumpets into fingers — or 'soldiers' for the more fanciful.

Spoon the fruit compote into four serving bowls and top with a generous spoonful of fromage frais. Stack the crumpet fingers on a side plate and serve.
Serves 4.

lemon grass creamed rice

110 g (1/2 cup) short-grain rice
1 litre (4 cups) milk
1 stem lemon grass, bruised
115 g (1/2 cup) caster (superfine) sugar
1 tsp natural vanilla extract
1 guava, sliced
1 small red papaya, sliced

Rinse the rice in a colander until the water runs clear. Drain well.

Pour the milk into a saucepan, add the lemon grass, sugar and vanilla and heat until the milk is about to boil. Add the rice and stir until the milk returns to the boil — this will take about 1 minute. Reduce the heat and now allow to simmer for an hour, stirring occasionally, until the rice is tender. Lift out the lemon grass.

Divide the rice among four bowls and top with the sliced fruit. Serve without delay so the rice stays tender.
Serves 4–6.

Wake up in wonderland with a bowl of this exotic rice pudding. Creamy, tender and soothing, every lingering spoonful offers an uplifting whiff of lemon grass to gently waken the senses.

little bites

tasty nibbles to
tide you over

Keep a sharp eye out for straying fingers while you make these irresistible fritters or they'll be snaffled up long before they hit the table.

corn fritters

6 fresh corn cobs or 325 g (11¹/₂ oz)
can corn kernels, drained
4 spring onions (scallions), finely chopped
1 garlic clove, crushed
1 tsp curry powder
2 tbs self-raising flour
1 tsp soy sauce
1 free-range egg
4 tbs oil
sweet chilli sauce (optional)

If you're using fresh corn, remove the kernels by carefully slicing down the length of the cobs with a sharp knife.

To make the batter for the fritters, gently mash together the corn kernels, spring onion, garlic, curry powder, flour, soy sauce and egg — a potato masher makes light work of this. Cover with plastic wrap and pop in the fridge for an hour.

When you're ready to eat, heat the oil in a large frying pan. Drop tablespoonfuls of the batter into the pan a few at a time, leaving some space between each fritter. Cook over medium heat for a few minutes on each side until golden brown all over — take care when turning the fritters so they don't break up. Remove from the pan, drain on paper towels and keep the fritters warm in a low oven while you cook up the rest. Serve with sweet chilli sauce or on their own.
Makes 12.

bruschetta

For the classic Tuscan topping:
6 ripe Roma (plum) tomatoes
15 g (1/2 cup) basil, shredded
1 garlic clove, finely chopped
2 tbs extra virgin olive oil

For the mushroom and parsley topping:
2 tbs olive oil
200 g (7 oz) small button mushrooms, quartered
1 tbs lemon juice
50 g (1 3/4 oz) goat's cheese, crumbled
1 tbs finely chopped flat-leaf (Italian) parsley
1 tsp thyme

16 thick slices of crusty white Italian-style bread
4 garlic cloves, halved
3 tbs olive oil

To make the classic Tuscan topping, first peel the tomatoes. The easiest way to do this is to score a cross in the base of each tomato and put them in a bowl of boiling water for 30 seconds, then plunge into cold water. The skin should peel away from the cross. Cut the tomatoes in half and scoop out the seeds with a teaspoon. Finely dice the flesh, then combine with the basil, garlic and oil.

To make the mushroom and parsley topping, heat the oil in a frying pan and gently fry the mushrooms until tender, about 5 minutes. Scoop into a small bowl, then stir in the lemon juice, goat's cheese, parsley and thyme.

Toast the bread and, while the slices are still hot, rub them with the cut side of a garlic clove. Drizzle olive oil over each slice, then season with salt and black pepper. Spread each topping over eight slices of bread and scoff the lot while they're still piping hot. Serves 8.

This classic Italian appetizer is perfect as a light lunch or easy snack. Make sure your tomatoes are really, really ripe, and don't skimp on the garlic — you'll find yourself licking your fingers all afternoon.

Who needs boring old chips and dips when you can whip up these delightful ricotta balls in no time at all? You can shape them in advance, then lazily cook them up as everyone gobbles them down.

ricotta balls with lemon dressing

500 g (2 cups) ricotta cheese
2 garlic cloves, chopped
3 tbs chopped chives
1 tbs finely grated lemon zest
20 g (1 cup) flat-leaf (Italian) parsley leaves
50 g (1/2 cup) grated Parmesan cheese,
plus some extra
1 free-range egg
75 g (3/4 cup) dry breadcrumbs
3 tbs olive oil
3 tbs pine nuts

For the lemon dressing:
2 tbs sugar
4 tbs lemon juice
5 fresh bay leaves, roughly torn

Put the ricotta, garlic, chives, lemon zest, parsley, Parmesan, egg and two-thirds of the breadcrumbs in a food processor and blitz until smooth.

Shape the ricotta mixture into 16 nicely sized balls and roll them around in the rest of the breadcrumbs. Now pop them into the freezer for 30 minutes — this will help keep them intact during cooking.

Heat the oil in a large frying pan and cook the ricotta balls over medium heat until golden all over, about 6 minutes. Add the pine nuts in the last minute of cooking — keep an eye on them so they don't burn! Remove the ricotta balls and pine nuts and keep them warm in a low oven while you make the dressing.

To make the lemon dressing, put the sugar, lemon juice and bay leaves in a saucepan with 170 ml (2/3 cup) water and bring to the boil. Reduce the heat and simmer for 5 minutes, or until reduced by half. Remove the bay leaves, then pour into a little bowl.

Serve the ricotta balls with a scattering of pine nuts and Parmesan, with the lemon dressing for dipping.
Makes 16.

tamari-roasted nut mix

250 g (9 oz) mixed nuts (we used
almonds, Brazil nuts, unsalted
peanuts and walnuts)
125 g (1 cup) pepitas (peeled pumpkin seeds)
125 g (1 cup) sunflower seeds
115 g (3/4 cup) cashews
120 g (3/4 cup) macadamias
125 ml (1/2 cup) tamari

Put all the nuts and seeds into a large bowl. Pour the tamari over them and toss together well, coating everything evenly. Now find something else to do while you let them stand for 10 minutes.

Spread the nut and seed mixture evenly over two large baking trays and bake for about 20 minutes in a 140°C (275°F/Gas 1) oven. Don't worry if the nuts don't seem crispy when you take them out of the oven — they will become crispy as they cool. Once they are completely cooled, you can store them in an airtight container for up to 2 weeks. Makes 750 g (4 cups).

When guests arrive for dinner, let them whet their appetites on this crunchy, munchy nut mix. Just make sure they leave some room for the main event!

Deliciously sustaining, this honey-powered snack deserves a permanent place in your emergency repertoire. Carry it with you and you'll never want for energy again.

puffed corn snack mix

175 g (6 oz) puffed corn
400 g (14 oz) dried fruit and nut mix
95 g (1¼ cups) unprocessed natural bran
55 g (1 cup) flaked coconut, toasted
4 tbs pepitas (peeled pumpkin seeds)
260 g (³/4 cup) honey

Combine all the dry ingredients in a large bowl and roughly mix them all together.

Heat the honey in a small saucepan over low heat until it is thin enough to be easily poured, about 3 minutes. Now pour the honey over the dry ingredients and stir well — it might be easier (and a whole lot messier!) to use your hands to make sure you get an even coating of honey over all the grains and nuts.

Spread a single layer of the mixture onto four baking trays lined with baking paper and bake in a 180°C (350°F/Gas 4) oven until golden, about 15 minutes. (If you don't have four baking trays, or can't fit four trays in your oven, cook the mixture in batches.) Turn the cereal several times during cooking so it doesn't burn. Cool completely, then store in an airtight container in a cool, dark place. Makes 20 serves.

spicy tempeh sticks

3 garlic cloves, coarsely chopped
4 spring onions (scallions), chopped
4 blanched almonds, chopped
1 tbs ground coriander
1/4 tsp cayenne pepper
1 tbs plain (all-purpose) flour
300 g (10 1/2 oz) block seasoned tempeh
oil, for deep-frying

Firstly, make a batter. Put the garlic, spring onions, almonds and 3 tablespoons water in a blender and blitz until almost smooth. Add the ground coriander, cayenne pepper, 1 teaspoon salt and 1/4 teaspoon pepper and blitz again until just combined. Scoop into a large bowl, then whisk in the flour.

Cut the tempeh lengthways into 2 x 6 cm (3/4 x 2 1/2 inch) strips, then cut in half again lengthways into large French-fry shapes.

Coat the tempeh sticks in the batter, then deep-fry in batches until golden brown and crisp. For the best results the oil should be 180°C (350°F). You can tell the temperature is right by dropping a cube of bread in the oil — if it browns in 15 seconds, the oil is perfect. When the tempeh sticks are done, remove them with a slotted spoon and drain on crumpled paper towels while you cook the rest. Serve while hot and crispy.
Serves 6–8.

Just like a futuristic super food, tempeh is crammed with all the good things and none of the bad. Tuck into it for protein, iron, calcium, zinc... Ooops, did we neglect to mention that it tastes fab, too?

Resist the temptation to buy a ready-made tub of tzatziki — this snappy version is light years ahead of the thin, sharp, over-processed goop that often bears the name.

tzatziki

2 Lebanese (short) cucumbers
400 g (14 oz) Greek-style yoghurt
4 garlic cloves, crushed
3 tbs finely chopped mint, plus a little extra
1 tbs lemon juice

The only trick to tzatziki is to prepare the cucumbers so they aren't watery. Leave the skin on, then cut them in half lengthways. Scoop out the seeds with a teaspoon and discard. Now coarsely grate the flesh into a small colander, sprinkle with a little salt and leave to stand over a large bowl for 15 minutes to drain off any bitter juices.

Meanwhile, find an attractive serving bowl and in it mix together the yoghurt, garlic, mint and lemon juice.

Back to the cucumber. Rinse well under cold water then, taking small handfuls, squeeze out the excess moisture. Stir the cucumber through the yoghurt mixture and season to taste. You could serve it straight away, or refrigerate for later use — either way, scatter with extra mint just before serving. Tzatziki is lovely served as a dip with flatbread, or as a sauce for spicy vegetable dishes. Makes 500 g (2 cups).

dolmades

200 g (7 oz) packet vine leaves in brine
220 g (1 cup) medium-grain rice
1 small onion, finely chopped
5 tbs pine nuts, toasted
2 tbs currants
2 tbs chopped dill
1 tbs finely chopped mint
1 tbs finely chopped flat-leaf (Italian) parsley
125 ml (1/2 cup) olive oil
2 tbs lemon juice
500 ml (2 cups) good-quality vegetable stock

Firstly, soak the vine leaves in cold water for 15 minutes, and in a separate bowl cover the rice with boiling water and soak for 15 minutes to soften. Drain them both. Pat the vine leaves dry and cut off any stems. Discard any leaves that look shabby, and keep some aside for lining the saucepan.

Combine the rice, onion, pine nuts, currants, herbs, 1 tablespoon of the olive oil and a little salt and pepper in a large bowl.

Lay a leaf vein-side down on a flat surface. Place a tablespoonful of filling in the centre. Fold the stalk end over, then fold the left and right sides into the centre, then roll firmly towards the tip into a small cigar shape. Repeat with the remaining filling and leaves.

Line the base of a large, heavy-based pan with the reserved vine leaves; drizzle with a little olive oil. Tightly pack the dolmades in the pan in a single layer, then pour the lemon juice, stock and the rest of the oil over them. Cover with an inverted plate, bring to the boil, then reduce the heat and simmer, covered, for 45 minutes. Remove with a slotted spoon and serve warm or cold with lemon wedges.
Makes 24.

When freshly made at home, these tasty parcels bear no comparison to their ready-made rivals. You could even try soaking some fresh vine leaves in salt water yourself — just ask your greengrocer to order some in for you.

Woefully misunderstood, lentils have been branded bland, boring hippy food — but nothing could be further from the truth. They hungrily soak up cooking flavours, which makes this dhal anything but dull.

dhal with pitta chips

2 tsp vegetable oil
1/2 onion, finely chopped
1 garlic clove, crushed
1/2 tsp cumin seeds
1/2 tsp ground coriander
1/2 tsp paprika
1/2 tsp garam masala
125 g (1/2 cup) red lentils
125 g (1/2 cup) canned chopped tomato
2 tbs roughly chopped coriander
(cilantro) leaves
2 wholemeal pitta pockets

Heat the oil in a saucepan over medium heat, then add the onion and cook until softened, about 5 minutes. Add the garlic and all the spices and cook very briefly until fragrant.

Now stir in those lovely lentils, then add 375 ml (1 1/2 cups) water and the tomato. Bring to the boil, reduce the heat and simmer for 15 minutes — we want the lentils to be very tender, and most of the liquid absorbed. Season to taste, scoop into a serving bowl and sprinkle with coriander leaves.

Meanwhile, make the pitta chips. First cut the pitta pockets open, so you have four circles. Cut each circle into eight wedges and lay out on a baking tray — we don't want them to overlap, so you may need to use a couple of trays. Bake in a 200°C (400°F/Gas 6) oven until crispy and golden, about 6 minutes. Allow the wedges to cool, then use them to scoop up the dhal.
Serves 4–6.

beetroot hummus

500 g (1 lb 2 oz) beetroot, trimmed
4 tbs olive oil
1 large onion, chopped
1 tbs ground cumin
400 g (14 oz) can chickpeas, drained
1 tbs tahini
4 tbs Greek-style yoghurt
3 garlic cloves, crushed
3 tbs lemon juice
125 ml (1/2 cup) vegetable stock

Scrub the beetroot well. Bring a pot of water to the boil, pop the beetroot in and cook over high heat until soft and cooked through, about 35 minutes.

Meanwhile, heat 1 tablespoon of the oil in a frying pan over medium heat and cook the onion until soft, about 5 minutes. Add the cumin and cook for a further minute until fragrant. Set aside for a while.

Drain the beetroot and let it cool slightly. Now pop on some gloves, hold the beetroot firmly in a kitchen towel and peel away the skin — this will keep your hands clean and save your fingers being burnt.

Roughly chop the beetroot flesh and put it in a food processor or blender with the onion mixture, chickpeas, tahini, yoghurt, garlic, lemon juice and stock and blitz until smooth. With the motor running, add the remaining oil in a thin steady stream. Keep blitzing until you have a thick, creamy mixture. Scoop the hummus into a pretty bowl and serve with Lebanese or Turkish bread. Makes 500 g (2 cups).

This intensely vivid dip is a real eye popper and palate pleaser. When peeling cooked beetroot, slip on a pair of rubber gloves, or your hands will be stained bright purple and you'll need to scrub, scrub, scrub…

Green tea is renowned as an antioxidant and is reputed to have cleansing properties. What better excuse do you need to tuck into these delicate rolls?

green tea sushi rolls

300 g (10$^1/_2$ oz) dried green tea soba noodles
6 sheets of roasted nori
50 g (1$^3/_4$ oz) pickled daikon, cut into long, thin strips
3 tbs drained red pickled ginger shreds
ready-made ponzu sauce, for dipping (ponzu sauce is made from rice vinegar, soy, mirin and dashi, and is sold in Japanese or Asian grocery stores)

Cook the noodles in a large saucepan of rapidly boiling water until tender, about 5 minutes. Rinse under cold water and pat dry with paper towels.

Working on a flat surface, lay one sheet of nori on a sushi mat. Put one-sixth of the noodles along the bottom half of the nori sheet, then arrange the daikon and pickled ginger along the centre of the noodles. Roll the nori up firmly to enclose the filling, then slice the roll into six pieces using a sharp knife. Repeat with the remaining ingredients. Arrange the nori rolls on a platter and serve with a little bowl of ponzu dipping sauce. Makes 36.

vegetable pakoras with spiced yoghurt

For the spiced yoghurt:
1 tsp cumin seeds
200 g (7 oz) Greek-style yoghurt
1 garlic clove, crushed
15 g (1/2 cup) coriander (cilantro)
leaves, chopped

For the batter:
4 tbs besan (chickpea flour)
4 tbs self-raising flour
4 tbs soy flour
1/2 tsp ground turmeric
1 tsp cayenne pepper
1/2 tsp ground coriander
1 small green chilli, seeded and
finely chopped

oil, for deep-frying
200 g (7 oz) cauliflower, cut into small florets
140 g (5 oz) orange sweet potato, peeled
and very thinly sliced
175 g (6 oz) eggplant (aubergine),
very thinly sliced
175 g (6 oz) fresh asparagus spears,
each cut into three lengths

Start with the spiced yoghurt. Heat a small frying pan over medium heat. Add the cumin seeds and dry-fry until aromatic — watch them carefully so they don't burn to a crisp. Tip the seeds into a mortar and pestle or spice grinder and roughly grind them up, then whisk them into the yoghurt with the garlic. Season with salt and freshly ground black pepper, then stir in the coriander leaves and scoop into a serving bowl.

Now make the batter. Put all the different flours into a bowl with the ground spices, chilli and 1 teaspoon salt. Gradually whisk in 250 ml (1 cup) cold water, then let the batter stand for 15 minutes.

Dip the vegetables in the batter and deep-fry in small batches for 1–2 minutes, or until pale gold. For the best results, the oil should be 170°C (325°F) — you'll know it's at the right temperature if a cube of bread dropped into the oil browns in 20 seconds. Remove the golden pakoras with a slotted spoon and drain on paper towels. Keep warm in a low oven until all the vegetables are deep-fried. Serve with the spiced yoghurt. Serves 4.

Party food for grown-ups, these nifty little numbers pack a spicy punch and will have your guests clamouring for more.

Crunchy on the outside, soft and yielding on the inside, nutty with sesame and salty with soy — these yummy little cubes are a mouthful of contradictions and are splendid on a cocktail party platter.

sesame-crusted tofu snacks

For the dipping sauce:
2 tbs light soy sauce
2 tbs mirin
1 tbs finely chopped fresh ginger

1¹/₂ tbs white sesame seeds
1¹/₂ tbs black sesame seeds
2 tbs cornflour (cornstarch)
300 g (10¹/₂ oz) firm tofu, cut into
2 cm (³/₄ inch) cubes
2 tbs oil

Firstly, make the dipping sauce. Simply put all the ingredients into a little serving bowl and mix together well.

On a plate, mix together all the sesame seeds and the cornflour, then season with salt and pepper and mix again. Gently toss the tofu in the sesame seed mixture to give it a spotty coating.

Now heat the oil in a large, heavy-based frying pan. Fry the tofu in batches over medium heat for 3–4 minutes, or until toasted on all sides — you'll need to turn the tofu frequently, and you might need to add a little more oil. Carefully remove and drain on paper towels.

Serve the tofu cubes with the dipping sauce, and supply some cocktail sticks so people can help themselves. Remember, no double dipping allowed!
Serves 4–6.

deep-fried zucchini flowers

12 zucchini (courgette) flowers
oil, for deep-frying
lemon wedges

For the batter:
5 tbs plain (all-purpose) flour
2 tsp olive oil
3 free-range egg whites

Check the zucchini flowers are clean and aren't harbouring any insects. Trim the stems to about 2 cm (3/4 inch) — this gives you something to hold on to when dipping the flowers into the batter.

To make the batter, sift the flour into a bowl and stir in 1/2 teaspoon salt. Mix in the oil with a wooden spoon, then slowly add 4–5 tablespoons warm water to make a smooth, thick batter. Whisk the egg whites until stiff peaks form, then gently fold them into the batter.

Dip the zucchini flowers into the batter, coating them completely. Deep-fry in batches until golden brown, about 2–3 minutes, turning once to cook both sides. Don't let the oil smoke — if it does, the oil is too hot.

Carefully remove the blossoms and drain on paper towels. Sprinkle with salt and enjoy at once with lemon wedges. If you want to prepare them a little in advance of serving, keep them warm in a low oven on a tray lined with crumpled greaseproof paper. Serves 4.

If you happen to grow zucchini at home, this is a brilliant way to use the sunny yellow flowers that proliferate throughout summer. To make them even more delectable, stuff them with a spoonful of mild, soft goat's cheese.

something light
a midday munch or midnight supper

Italian for 'green', verde is a vibrant emerald dressing that adds a piquant edge to these succulent kebabs. Presented on a plain white platter, these skewers are a riot of colour.

vegetable kebabs with salsa verde

For the salsa verde:

1 garlic clove
1 tbs capers, rinsed and squeezed dry
20 g (1 cup) flat-leaf (Italian) parsley
15 g (½ cup) basil leaves
10 g (½ cup) mint leaves
4 tbs olive oil
1 tsp Dijon mustard
1 tbs red wine vinegar

16 small yellow squash
16 French shallots, peeled
16 baby zucchini (courgettes)
16 baby carrots, peeled
1 large red capsicum (pepper), halved and cut into 2 cm (3/4 inch) thick slices
2 garlic cloves, crushed
1 tsp chopped thyme
1 tbs olive oil
16 bay or sage leaves

To avoid a fiery inferno, soak 16 bamboo skewers in cold water for 30 minutes before you start cooking.

To make the salsa verde, briefly blitz the garlic, capers and herbs in a food processor. With the motor running, pour in the olive oil in a slow, steady stream until just mixed through, then scoop into a bowl. Now combine the mustard with the red wine vinegar and stir it through the salsa verde. Season, cover with plastic wrap and keep in the fridge until needed.

Blanch the vegetables in separate batches in a large pot of boiling, salted water until just tender. Drain in a colander, then toss with the garlic, thyme and oil. Season well.

Thread the vegetables onto the skewers, starting with a squash, then a French shallot, a bay or sage leaf, then a zucchini, carrot and capsicum slice. You should have enough vegetables to make 16 skewers.

You can fry the skewers on a chargrill pan (griddle) or barbecue hotplate for 3 minutes on each side, or cook them under a griller (broiler) for the same amount of time. Arrange on a bed of couscous or rice and serve with a dollop of salsa verde.
Serves 4.

sweet and sour dhal

500 g (1 lb 2 oz) yellow lentils
5 x 5 cm (2 x 2 inch) piece of kokum
2 tsp coriander seeds
2 tsp cumin seeds
2 tbs oil
2 tsp black mustard seeds
10 curry leaves
7 cloves
10 cm (4 inch) cinnamon stick
5 green chillies, finely chopped
1/2 tsp ground turmeric
400 g (14 oz) can chopped tomatoes
15 g (1/2 oz) jaggery or 10 g (1/4 oz) molasses
coriander (cilantro) leaves

Soak the lentils in cold water for 2 hours. Rinse the kokum well and soak in cold water for a few minutes to soften. Drain the lentils and place in a heavy-based saucepan with 1 litre (4 cups) of water and the kokum. Slowly bring to the boil, then reduce the heat and simmer for about 40 minutes, or until the lentils are tender.

In a small frying pan over low heat, dry-roast the coriander seeds until aromatic. Remove, then dry-roast the cumin seeds. Grind the roasted seeds to a fine powder using a spice grinder or mortar and pestle. What a wild aroma!

Heat the oil in a small pan over low heat. Add the mustard seeds and let them pop. Add the curry leaves, cloves, cinnamon stick, chilli, turmeric and the roasted spice mix and cook for 1 minute.

Throw in the tomatoes and cook until soft enough to mush into the sauce, about 2–3 minutes. Now add the jaggery, then pour the whole spicy mixture into the simmering lentils and cook for 10 minutes. Check for salt, then sprinkle with coriander leaves and serve with plenty of rice, some vegetables and maybe some naan bread. Serves 8.

Toor, kokum and jaggery: not a firm of lawyers but essential ingredients in this sweet and sour dhal. Toor is yellow lentil, kokum an acidic fruit reminiscent of tamarind, and jaggery a dark palm sugar. Ask for them in an Asian or Indian food store.

A good bouquet garni lends a gentle, complex tenor to this fresh vegetable soup; pesto makes it positively sing. The flavours are even better if the soup is made a day ahead, then gently reheated.

vegetable soup with pesto

3 stalks of flat-leaf (Italian) parsley
1 large sprig of rosemary
1 large sprig of thyme
1 large sprig of marjoram
3 tbs olive oil
2 onions, thinly sliced
1 leek, thinly sliced
1 bay leaf
375 g (13 oz) pumpkin, peeled and cut into small pieces
250 g (9 oz) potato, peeled and cut into small pieces
1 carrot, thinly sliced
2 litres (8 cups) vegetable stock or water
80 g (1/2 cup) fresh or frozen broad (fava) beans
80 g (1/2 cup) fresh or frozen peas
2 small zucchinis (courgettes), finely chopped
2 ripe tomatoes, peeled and roughly chopped
60 g (1/2 cup) short macaroni or shell pasta

For the pesto:
25 g (3/4 cup) basil
2 large garlic cloves, crushed
4 tbs olive oil
4 tbs grated Parmesan cheese

Make a bouquet garni by tying the parsley, rosemary, thyme and marjoram together with kitchen string.

Heat the oil in a heavy-based saucepan and fry the onion and leek over medium heat until soft and lightly golden, about 10 minutes. Add the bouquet garni, bay leaf, pumpkin, potato, carrot, stock and 1 teaspoon of salt, then pop the lid on and simmer until the vegies are almost tender, about 10 minutes.

Now add the broad beans, peas, zucchini, tomato and pasta. Pop the lid back on and simmer until the vegetables are very tender and the pasta is cooked, about 15 minutes. Add a little water if the soup looks too thick. Remove the bouquet garni and bay leaf.

To make the pesto, briefly whiz the basil and garlic in a food processor until roughly chopped — or use a mortar and pestle, if you prefer. Gradually pour in the oil, blitzing (or pounding) until smooth, then stir in the Parmesan and 1/2 teaspoon freshly ground black pepper. Serve each bowl of soup with a dollop of pesto.
Serves 8.

herbed omelettes

15 g (1¹/₂ tbs) butter
2 French shallots, finely chopped
1 garlic clove, crushed
2 tbs chopped parsley
2 tbs chopped basil
2 tsp chopped tarragon
2 tbs thick (double/heavy) cream
8 fresh free-range eggs, lightly beaten
oil, for pan-frying

Melt the butter in a frying pan and fry the shallots and garlic over low heat until tender, about 3 minutes. Stir in the herbs, then tip into a bowl and allow to cool. Mix in the cream and beaten eggs and season well.

Heat a little oil in a non-stick frying pan. Pour a quarter of the omelette mixture into the pan and cook on low to medium heat, constantly pulling the set egg around the edge of the pan into the centre, until the omelette is set and golden underneath and the top is just cooked — this might take about 3–4 minutes. Now fold two sides of the omelette into the centre to form an oblong shape. Place a plate on top, then gently invert so the seam of the omelette sits underneath. Serve hot for someone to start on while you cook the other three omelettes. Serves 4.

An omelette is incredibly easy to cook, and so very versatile. Leave one herb out, use others instead, add some tomatoes, mushrooms, goat's cheese — whatever you fancy, really...

If a food could be said to taste green, pesto is it — especially fresh pesto, and particularly when it's coating a cornucopia of fresh green vegetables!

pasta with pesto and summer vegetables

500 g (1 lb 2 oz) penne
200 g (7 oz) fresh or frozen shelled broad (fava) beans
200 g (7 oz) fresh or frozen shelled peas
310 g (2 bunches) fresh asparagus spears, cut into 4 cm (1¹/₂ inch) lengths
4 tbs good-quality pesto, or use the recipe on page 87
2 tbs lemon juice
2 tbs extra virgin olive oil
4 tbs grated Parmesan cheese

Cook the pasta in a large pot of boiling salted water until *al dente*.

Meanwhile, steam all the vegetables until tender, which should only take 4 minutes. Keep them warm while you peel the skin from the broad beans.

If you're using ready-made pesto, whisk it up with the lemon juice and olive oil to revive the flavour — if you've made your own, you won't need to add more oil.

Now drain the pasta and toss together with the steamed vegetables. Season with salt and pepper, drizzle with the pesto, scatter with Parmesan and serve without delay.
Serves 4.

soya bean and mushroom burgers

2 tbs oil
1 onion, finely chopped
200 g (7 oz) field or cap mushrooms,
finely chopped
1 garlic clove, crushed
425 g (15 oz) can soya beans,
rinsed and drained
120 g (1 1/2 cups) fresh
wholemeal breadcrumbs
2 tsp thyme, chopped
1 free-range egg, lightly beaten
4 Turkish bread rolls
1 avocado, mashed
mixed lettuce leaves
ready-made tomato chutney

Heat 2 teaspoons of the oil in a frying pan, then gently fry the onion for a few minutes until softened but not browned. Add the mushrooms and garlic and cook until just soft, about 2 minutes. Leave to cool slightly.

Meanwhile, put the soya beans in a large bowl and roughly mash with a potato masher. Add the mushroom mixture, breadcrumbs, thyme and beaten egg. Season well with salt and freshly ground black pepper and stir until well combined. With wet hands, shape the mixture into four patties about 10 cm (4 inches) in diameter.

Now heat the rest of the oil in a frying pan. Cook the patties a few at a time over medium heat until golden brown and heated through — they'll take about 2–3 minutes each side. They will be quite fragile, so handle them carefully.

To assemble the burgers, split the rolls and toast on both sides. Spread the base with the mashed avocado, then top with the lettuce, a soya patty and a dollop of chutney. Pop the toasted lid on top and enjoy!
Serves 4.

Sometimes only a burger will do — and with one of these in your belly you'll be ready to take on the world. Made from hearty mushrooms and creamy beans, these burgers offer mountains of taste trapped in a toasted Turkish roll.

Like Fred Astaire and Ginger Rogers, Bogie and Bacall, Mickey and Minnie, some pairs belong together. Let carrot and ginger join the rollcall of perfect partners. Start this dish the night before to let them do their thing.

tofu with carrot and ginger sauce

600 g (1 lb 5 oz) firm tofu, drained
and cut into 12 even slices
125 ml ($1/2$ cup) orange juice
1 tbs soft brown sugar
1 tbs soy sauce
2 tbs chopped coriander (cilantro) leaves
2 garlic cloves, crushed
1 tsp grated fresh ginger
2–3 tbs oil
1 kg (2 lb 4 oz) baby bok choy (pak choi),
cut into quarters lengthways

For the carrot and ginger sauce:
300 g ($10^{1/2}$ oz) carrots, chopped
2 tsp grated fresh ginger
170 ml ($2/3$ cup) orange juice
125 ml ($1/2$ cup) vegetable stock

Lay the tofu slices in a single layer in a flat, non-metallic dish. Mix together the orange juice, brown sugar, soy sauce, coriander, garlic and ginger, then pour it over the tofu. Cover and keep in the fridge overnight.

Drain the tofu, but keep the marinade. Heat the oil in a large frying pan and fry the tofu in batches over medium high heat until golden, about 1–2 minutes each side. Remove and keep warm while you fry the rest of the tofu. When you're done, bring the marinade to the boil, then reduce the heat and simmer for 1 minute. Keep in a warm place.

Steam the bok choy until wilted; keep warm.

Now put all the carrot and ginger sauce ingredients in a saucepan. Bring to the boil, then reduce the heat, pop a lid on and simmer until the carrot is tender, about 5 minutes. Scoop the sauce into a food processor or blender and blitz until smooth.

Divide the bok choy among six plates. Top with some carrot and ginger sauce, then some tofu, and drizzle on a little of the marinade before serving.
Serves 6.

artichoke frittata

175 g (6 oz) broad (fava) beans,
fresh or frozen
400 g (14 oz) can artichoke hearts, drained
3 tbs olive oil
1 onion, thinly sliced
6 free-range eggs
2 tbs chopped parsley
50 g (1 3/4 oz) pecorino cheese, grated
pinch of freshly grated nutmeg

Boil the broad beans in a pot of lightly salted water for 2 minutes, then drain and rinse under cold water. Now slip the skins off the beans.

Cut the artichoke hearts from bottom to top into slices about 5 mm (1/4 inch) wide. Throw away any bits that contain the tough central choke.

Heat the oil in a 30 cm (12 inch) frying pan and gently fry the onion over low heat for a few minutes until softened but not browned. Add the artichoke and cook for 1–2 minutes, then stir in the broad beans.

Lightly beat together the eggs, parsley, pecorino and nutmeg, then season well with salt and pepper. Pour into the frying pan and cook over low heat until the egg is almost set, shaking the pan often to stop the frittata sticking. Finish the top off under a hot grill (broiler), and leave to cool before serving in wedges.
Serves 4.

The granddaddy of the thistle family, the artichoke's intimidating armour hides the tender heart within. The outer leaves take a bit of effort to negotiate, so take the easy option and buy the succulent hearts from your local deli.

This is really just an elegant version of cheese on toast — brilliant when you couldn't be bothered fiddle-faddling about in the kitchen but you're hungry for a flavour hit. Close your eyes, take a deep bite and let yourself be spirited off to a rustic Greek island.

haloumi with salad and garlic bread

4 firm, ripe tomatoes
1 Lebanese (short) cucumber
140 g (5 oz) rocket (arugula)
80 g ($\frac{1}{2}$ cup) Kalamata olives
1 loaf crusty white bread, cut into
8 thick slices
125 ml ($\frac{1}{2}$ cup) olive oil
1 large garlic clove, cut in half
400 g (14 oz) haloumi cheese, cut into 8 slices
1 tbs lemon juice
1 tbs chopped oregano

Cut the tomatoes and cucumber into nice bite-sized chunks. Toss them into your most attractive salad bowl with the rocket and olives, and mix well.

Drizzle the bread slices with a little of the olive oil and season with salt and pepper. Toast lightly under a hot grill (broiler), then roughly rub the cut side of the garlic all over the toast. Wrap loosely in foil and keep warm in a low oven.

Heat 2 teaspoons of the oil in a shallow frying pan and fry the haloumi over high heat for 1–2 minutes on each side, until crisp and golden brown.

Whisk together the lemon juice, oregano and remaining olive oil (you'll need about 3 tablespoons) to use as a dressing. Season to taste. Now simply pour half the dressing over the salad, toss well, arrange the fried haloumi on top and drizzle with the rest of the dressing. Serve with the warm garlic bread and tuck in straight away.
Serves 4.

marinated grilled tofu salad with ginger miso dressing

4 tbs tamari or Japanese soy sauce
4 tsp oil
2 garlic cloves, crushed
1 tsp grated fresh ginger
1 tsp chilli paste
500 g (1 lb 2 oz) firm tofu, cut into
2 cm (3/4 inch) cubes
400 g (14 oz) mesclun leaves
1 Lebanese (short) cucumber, thinly sliced
250 g (1 punnet) cherry tomatoes, halved

For the dressing:
2 tsp white miso paste
2 tbs mirin
1 tsp sesame oil
1 tsp grated fresh ginger
1 tsp finely chopped chives
1 tbs toasted sesame seeds

Mix together the tamari, 2 teaspoons of the oil, the garlic, ginger and chilli paste in a bowl with 1/2 teaspoon salt. Add the tofu and mix until well coated. Marinate for at least 10 minutes, or preferably overnight.

To make the dressing, combine the miso with 125 ml (1/2 cup) hot water and leave until the miso dissolves. Add the mirin, sesame oil, ginger, chives and sesame seeds and stir thoroughly until the mixture starts to thicken.

Combine the mesclun, cucumber and cherry tomatoes in a serving bowl, ready to go.

Drain the tofu, but don't throw away the delicious marinade. Heat the rest of the oil on a chargrill pan (griddle) or barbecue hotplate. Add the tofu and cook over high heat until golden brown on all sides, which will take about 4 minutes. Pour on the reserved marinade and cook for another minute over high heat. Remove the tofu, let it cool for 5 minutes, then add it to the salad. Drizzle with the dressing, toss well and enjoy without delay.
Serves 4.

That the humble soya bean can produce a paste as complex and delicate as miso is something we should all be thankful for. And that it is so very good for you is a minor miracle of nature.

Baby rocket leaves are milder than their older siblings, but still pack a peppery punch. Here they pep up a plain pizza base faster than you can say pickled peppers!

✓ super salad pizza

4 ready-made individual thick pizza bases
2 tbs tomato paste (purée)
2 tsp chopped oregano
75 g (1/2 cup) feta cheese, crumbled
100 g (2/3 cup) grated mozzarella cheese
65 g (2/3 cup) grated Parmesan cheese
100 g (3 1/2 oz) baby rocket (arugula),
trimmed
3 tbs flat-leaf (Italian) parsley
1/4 small red onion, thinly sliced
3 tbs olive oil
1 tbs lemon juice
1 tsp Dijon mustard
50 g (1/2 cup) shaved Parmesan cheese

Put the pizza bases on a baking tray — use two trays if you need to. Spread the bases with tomato paste, then sprinkle with the oregano, feta and grated cheeses. Bake in a 200°C (400°F/Gas 6) oven for about 12 minutes, or until the cheese is bubbling.

Meanwhile, grab a bowl and toss in the rocket, parsley and onion. Whisk together the oil, lemon juice and mustard, then splash it all through the salad.

Top the hot pizza bases with the salad and sprinkle with shaved Parmesan. Enjoy straight away while the pizzas are piping hot.
Serves 4.

caramelized leek, goat's cheese and spinach tart

For the pastry:
250 g (2 cups) plain (all-purpose) flour
125 g (4^1/$_2$ oz) butter
3–4 tbs iced water

For the filling:
2 tbs olive oil
1 leek, thinly sliced
1 fennel bulb, thinly sliced
150 g (3 cups) baby English spinach
75 g (1/2 cup) crumbled goat's cheese
3 free-range eggs, lightly beaten
170 ml (2/3 cup) cream

To make the pastry, put the flour and butter in a food processor and blitz briefly until the mixture looks like breadcrumbs. Keep the motor running and gradually add the iced water until the pastry comes together. Gather into a ball, cover with plastic wrap and refrigerate for 20 minutes.

Roll the pastry out on a lightly floured surface to fit a 22 cm (8^1/$_2$ inch) fluted flan tin. Ease the pastry into the tin and trim off any excess so you'll have a nice neat tart. Line the pastry with baking paper and fill with baking weights or rice. Bake in a 200°C (400°F/Gas 6) oven for 15 minutes, then remove the weights and the paper and bake for a further 10 minutes. Reduce the oven temperature to 160°C (315°F/Gas 2–3).

While the pastry is blind baking, heat the oil in a frying pan, add the leek and fennel and cook over medium heat until the leeks are caramelized, about 20 minutes. Take the pan off the heat; add the spinach and let it wilt. Now spread the mixture over the pastry shell and top with the goat's cheese. Combine the eggs and cream, pour into the pastry shell and bake until set, about 40 minutes. Serves 6.

This continental bistro classic is a cinch to make at home. The trick to producing perfect pastry is cold, cold, cold. Chill your implements, your butter, even your hands, and work the dough as little as possible.

If you love a little heat in your life, add the diced flesh of two small green or red chillies to the salsa to give these patties extra bite.

spiced soya bean patties with salsa

For the salsa:
1 cucumber, seeded and diced
1 tomato, seeded and diced
1/4 red onion, finely chopped
1 tbs chopped coriander (cilantro) leaves
1 tbs chopped mint
2 tbs olive oil
1 tbs white wine vinegar

For the patties:
1/2 tsp finely grated lemon zest
1 tbs lemon juice
600 g (1 lb 5 oz) can soya beans, rinsed and drained
4 tbs roughly chopped flat-leaf (Italian) parsley
60 g (3/4 cup) fresh breadcrumbs
2 tsp ground cumin
2 tsp ground coriander
3/4 tsp paprika
2 tbs olive oil

Combine all the salsa ingredients in a little serving bowl and stir together well. Season.

To make the patties, put the lemon zest, lemon juice, soya beans and parsley in a food processor and blitz in bursts until roughly mashed. Scoop the mixture into a large bowl and add the breadcrumbs, ground cumin, ground coriander and paprika — get your hands in there and mix it all together. Now wet your hands and divide the mixture into four portions. Shape into patties 8 cm (3 inches) in diameter.

Now heat the oil in a large frying pan over medium heat and fry the patties — two at a time, if necessary — until golden on both sides, about 2–3 minutes each side. Serve with plenty of crusty bread and a generous scoop of salsa.
Serves 4.

roasted tomatoes and eggplant with red lentil purée

For the balsamic vinaigrette:
3 tbs extra virgin olive oil
1 tbs balsamic vinegar

500 g (1 lb 2 oz) eggplant (aubergine),
thickly sliced
700 g (1 lb 9 oz) Roma (plum) tomatoes,
halved lengthways
150 g (5½ oz) rocket (arugula)
3 tbs pine nuts, toasted

For the red lentil purée:
625 ml (2½ cups) vegetable stock
200 g (7 oz) red lentils
1 tsp paprika
1 garlic clove, crushed

The vinaigrette is a cinch: simply whisk the oil and vinegar together with a large pinch each of salt and freshly ground black pepper.

Line a baking tray with foil, then lightly oil it. Arrange the eggplant and tomatoes, cut-sides facing up, on the tray, then brush them with 1 tablespoon of the balsamic vinaigrette. Bake in a 180°C (350°F/Gas 4) oven for 40 minutes, then transfer the eggplant to a plate and keep warm. Pop the tomatoes back in the oven for another 30 minutes, or until they start to brown on the edges.

While the tomatoes are baking, make the lentil purée. Pour the stock into a pot and bring to the boil. Add the lentils and paprika, return to the boil, then reduce the heat and simmer for 10 minutes, so the lentils become tender. Add a tablespoon of the balsamic vinaigrette, then add the garlic and stir pretty constantly for 5 minutes until the lentils break up and form a thick purée. Season with salt and pepper.

Scoop the lentil purée into six serving bowls. Top with the rocket leaves, then some roasted eggplant and tomato. Drizzle with the rest of the balsamic vinaigrette and sprinkle with pine nuts. Serve with crusty bread to scoop up all that lovely lentil purée.
Serves 6.

To truly inspire and transport us, food must seduce the eye, the nose, the palate. Let this spicy warm ensemble whisk you off somewhere sensuous and hot on a cold and dreary afternoon.

This superb strudel is sensational picnic fare. Prepare it the night before so you can enjoy it at your leisure with a glass or two of verdelho or other dry white wine.

rainbow strudel

1 tbs olive oil
1 onion, finely chopped
1/2 red capsicum (pepper), thinly sliced
6 thin slices of pumpkin, peeled
1 zucchini (courgette), sliced lengthways
8 button mushrooms, sliced
12 English spinach leaves
12 fresh asparagus spears, cut into thirds
6 sheets of filo pastry
light olive oil, to brush
40 g (1/2 cup) fresh breadcrumbs
sesame seeds, to sprinkle

For the vinaigrette:
100 ml (31/2 fl oz) extra virgin olive oil
11/2 tbs balsamic vinegar
1 ripe tomato, peeled, seeded and diced
1 tbs chopped basil

Heat the oil in a frying pan over medium heat and cook the onion and capsicum for 2 minutes. Add the pumpkin, zucchini and mushrooms and cook, stirring now and then, until the mushroom stalks soften, about 3 minutes. Remove from the heat, add the spinach and asparagus and toss well.

Lay a sheet of pastry on a workbench, brush with a little oil and sprinkle with 2 tablespoons of the breadcrumbs. Top with another sheet of pastry and repeat the process until you have used up all the pastry.

Heat a baking tray in a 220°C (425°F/Gas 7) oven for 5 minutes. Drain any excess juice from the vegetable mixture, then spoon the mixture in a row down one long edge of pastry, leaving a thin border. Now roll up the strudel lengthways, carefully lift onto the hot baking tray and tuck in the edges. Brush with a little oil and sprinkle with sesame seeds. Bake until lightly golden, about 20 minutes.

Now for the finishing touch. Put all the vinaigrette ingredients in a screw-top jar, season well, give it a good shake, and serve with the strudel.
Serves 4.

crisp polenta with mushrooms

1 litre (4 cups) vegetable stock
150 g (1 cup) polenta (cornmeal)
40 g (2 tbs) butter
1 tbs grated fresh Parmesan cheese
some rocket (arugula)
shavings of fresh Parmesan cheese

For the mushroom sauce:
10 g (1/4 oz) dried porcini mushrooms
1 tbs olive oil
800 g (1 lb 12 oz) mixed mushrooms
(we used field and Swiss browns),
thickly sliced
4 garlic cloves, finely chopped
2 tsp chopped thyme
185 ml (3/4 cup) dry white wine
125 ml (1/2 cup) vegetable stock
30 g (1/2 cup) chopped parsley

In a large saucepan, bring the stock to the boil. Add the polenta in a thin stream, stirring constantly, then quickly reduce the heat so the stock is simmering. Stir like a demon for the first 30 seconds, so no lumps appear — then you can let it mildly bubble away for 20 minutes, stirring every few minutes to stop it sticking, until the polenta starts to leave the sides of the pan. Add the butter, Parmesan, salt and pepper and mix well. Pour into a lightly greased shallow 20 cm (8 inch) square cake tin. Smooth the surface, then refrigerate for 30 minutes to let it set.

To make the mushroom sauce, soak the porcini in 125 ml (1/2 cup) boiling water for 10 minutes. Drain, reserving 4 tablespoons of the liquid. Heat the oil in a large frying pan and cook the mixed mushrooms over high heat until softened, about 5 minutes. Add the porcini, garlic and thyme, then season and cook for a few more minutes. Splash in the wine and cook until it has evaporated. Pour in the stock, then reduce the heat and cook for a few minutes until the stock has reduced and thickened. Stir in the parsley.

Cut the polenta into four squares and cook under a hot grill (broiler) until golden on both sides. Divide among four serving plates and top with the mushrooms, some rocket and Parmesan shavings — dig in, don't wait. Serves 4.

Rich, earthy and complex, porcini are the princes of the mushroom world. Their name translates as 'piglet' — and it's certainly easy to make a pig of yourself eating them.

Defiantly, pungently hot, wasabi demands to be treated with respect. Go as hot as you dare with the mayonnaise — just make sure you warn your guests, and keep the drinks table stocked with water!

tempura vegetables with wasabi mayonnaise

For the wasabi mayonnaise:
2 tbs whole-egg mayonnaise
3 tsp wasabi paste
1/2 tsp grated lime zest

2 free-range egg yolks
250 ml (1 cup) chilled soda water
3 tbs cornflour (cornstarch)
115 g (4 oz) plain (all-purpose) flour
3 tbs sesame seeds, toasted
oil, for deep-frying
1 small eggplant (aubergine), cut into
5 mm (1/4 inch) rounds
1 large onion, cut into 5 mm (1/4 inch)
rounds, rings intact
300 g (10 1/2 oz) orange sweet potato, peeled
and cut into 5 mm (1/4 inch) rounds

First, make the wasabi mayonnaise: simply mix all the ingredients together in a small serving bowl. Keep in the fridge covered with plastic wrap until you're ready to serve.

The secret to tempura is in the batter: it should be made just before you want to cook, and be mixed as briefly as possible, leaving the batter lumpy (yes, lumpy!).

Combine the egg yolks and soda water in a jug, and mix lightly with a whisk. Sift the cornflour and flour into a bowl, then add the sesame seeds and a good sprinkling of salt and mix well. Pour in the soda water mixture and stir lightly with chopsticks or a fork until just combined but still lumpy.

Fill a deep heavy-based saucepan or wok one-third full of oil and heat until a cube of bread dropped into the oil browns in 15 seconds. Dip the vegetables into the batter and cook in batches for 3–4 minutes, or until golden brown and cooked through. Drain on crumpled paper towels and sprinkle generously with salt. Keep warm but don't cover, or the tempura will go soggy. Transfer to a warmed serving platter and serve straight away with the wasabi mayonnaise. Serves 4–6.

asparagus soup with parmesan crisps

700 g (1 lb 9 oz) fresh asparagus
spears, trimmed
1 tbs vegetable oil
30 g (1½ tbs) butter
1 large red onion, finely chopped
1 large leek, thinly sliced
2 large potatoes, peeled and cut into
1 cm (½ inch) cubes
1.25 litres (5 cups) good-quality
vegetable stock
4 tbs cream
4 tbs sour cream
1 tbs snipped chives

For the Parmesan crisps:
65 g (⅔ cup) grated Parmesan cheese

Roughly chop 600 g (1 lb 5 oz) of the asparagus, reserving the tips. Heat the oil and butter in a large saucepan over medium heat and cook the onion and leek until soft, about 5 minutes. Add the potato, chopped asparagus and stock and bring to the boil. Reduce the heat and simmer until the vegetables are tender, about 10 minutes. Blanch the asparagus tips in a saucepan of boiling water, then refresh in cold water.

Meanwhile, make the Parmesan crisps. Put four 9 cm (3½ inch) egg rings on a lined baking tray. Sprinkle about a tablespoon of the Parmesan into each ring in a thin layer — for a lacy edge, remove the rings, otherwise leave the rings in place. Bake in a 190°C (375°F/Gas 5) oven for 5 minutes, or until melted and just golden brown. Repeat with the rest of the Parmesan until you have 12 crisps. Cool before serving.

Let the soup cool a little, then pour it into a blender or food processor and blitz until nicely puréed. Pour the soup back into the pan, then stir in the cream and let it gently heat through. Season with salt and pepper, then ladle the soup into four bowls. Top with some sour cream, asparagus tips and chives, and serve with the Parmesan crisps. Serves 4.

These Parmesan crisps are so moreish that you should whip up an extra batch for munching in front of the telly later on. The asparagus soup is delicious too.

With an alcohol content of up to 13%, mirin is a pantry staple with a spirited secret — but we definitely don't recommend it as a kitchen tipple! Here it gives those spicy green beans a dash of something extra.

spicy green beans with toasted almonds and rice

3 tbs sesame oil
500 g (2 1/2 cups) jasmine rice
1 long red chilli, seeded and finely chopped
2 cm (3/4 inch) piece of fresh ginger,
peeled and grated
2 garlic cloves, crushed
375 g (13 oz) green beans, trimmed
and cut into 5 cm (2 inch) lengths
125 ml (1/2 cup) hoisin sauce
1 tbs soft brown sugar
2 tbs mirin
250 g (9 oz) toasted almonds,
roughly chopped

Heat 1 tablespoon of the sesame oil in a 1.5 litre (6 cup) flameproof casserole dish. Add the rice and stir over medium heat until all the grains are coated with oil, then pour in 1 litre (4 cups) boiling water. Stir well, pop the lid on and bake in a 200°C (400°F/Gas 6) oven for 20 minutes, so all the water is absorbed and the rice is tender. Keep warm.

Meanwhile, heat the rest of the oil in a wok or large frying pan. Briefly cook the chilli, ginger and garlic over high heat until lightly browned. Add the beans, hoisin sauce and sugar and stir-fry for 2 minutes. Splash in the mirin and cook for another minute — the aim is for the beans to be tender but still crunchy. Remove from the heat, stir in the almonds, and serve on a bed of the baked rice.
Serves 4–6.

miso soup with udon and tofu

1 tsp dashi granules
3 tbs red miso paste
2 tbs soy sauce
400 g (14 oz) fresh udon noodles, separated
400 g (14 oz) silken firm tofu, cubed
100 g (3½ oz) fresh shiitake
mushrooms, sliced
375 g (1 bunch) baby bok choy (pak choi),
leaves separated

Find a large saucepan and throw in the dashi, miso, soy sauce and 1.25 litres (5 cups) water. Bring to the boil, then reduce the heat and simmer for 10 minutes.

Add the noodles and cook until soft, about 5 minutes. Stir in the tofu, mushrooms and bok choy and let the broth bubble away until the bok choy wilts, about 3 minutes. Ladle into serving bowls and slurp to your heart's content.
Serves 2–4.

Few of us have the skills to emulate a master sushi chef, but even the clumsiest kitchen klutz can pull off this classic Japanese home-style dish of thick, hearty noodles in a delicate miso broth.

Winter just isn't winter without a bowl of heartwarming tomato soup. Keep a vast vat of it in the fridge to heat up on chilly, wet afternoons.

tomato soup

1.5 kg (3 lb 5 oz) Roma (plum) tomatoes,
halved lengthways
2 tsp chopped thyme
1 tsp sea salt
2 1/2 tbs olive oil
2 onions, chopped
4 large garlic cloves, crushed
1/4 tsp chilli flakes
400 g (14 oz) can tomatoes
1.5 litres (6 cups) vegetable stock
15 g (1/2 cup) basil, torn
1 tbs balsamic vinegar
pinch of sugar

Put the tomatoes on a large, lined baking tray with the cut-sides facing up. Sprinkle with the thyme and sea salt, drizzle with 1 1/2 tablespoons of the oil, then roast in a 200°C (400°F/Gas 6) oven for an hour.

Heat the rest of the oil in a saucepan over medium heat. Sauté the onion until soft and starting to brown — 10 minutes or so. Add the garlic and cook briefly, then toss in the roasted tomatoes (including any delicious cooking juices), along with the chilli flakes, canned tomatoes, stock and basil. Bring to the boil, then reduce the heat, pop the lid on and simmer for 40 minutes.

Let the soup cool slightly, then blitz it in a food processor or blender until smooth. Scoop it back into the cleaned pan and stir in the vinegar. Taste the soup and add a pinch of sugar if you think it needs it. Serve steaming hot — and feel it doing you good! Serves 4–6.

salt and pepper tofu puffs

125 ml (1/2 cup) sweet chilli sauce
2 tbs lemon juice
250 g (2 cups) cornflour (cornstarch)
2 tbs salt
1 tbs ground white pepper
2 tsp caster (superfine) sugar
2 x 200 g (7 oz) packets fried tofu puffs, cut in half and patted dry
4 free-range egg whites, lightly beaten
oil, for deep-frying
lemon wedges

Start by mixing together the sweet chilli sauce and lemon juice to make a dipping sauce.

Make a batter for the tofu by mixing the cornflour, salt, pepper and caster sugar together in a large bowl. Working in batches, dip the tofu puffs into the egg white (this will help the batter stick to the tofu), then toss them about in the salt and pepper mixture.

Fill a deep heavy-based saucepan or wok one-third full of oil and heat until a cube of bread dropped into the oil browns in 15 seconds. Cook the tofu in batches until crisp and golden, about 2 minutes. Drain well on crumpled paper towels and serve with the dipping sauce while crispy and hot. Serves 4–6.

There's really nothing at all to deep-frying food. The trick is to get the temperature right. Make sure the oil is hot, just don't let it smoke — we certainly don't want these yummy little puffs going up in puffs of smoke!

Deliciously fresh and never, ever greasy, a Vietnamese spring roll holds a universe of flavour. Balance is the key, so all the flavours jostle for favour, without overwhelming each other.

vietnamese spring rolls

70 g (2¹/₂ oz) dried rice vermicelli
200 g (7 oz) firm tofu
1 tsp sesame oil
1 tbs peanut oil
1 packet 15 cm (6 inch) square
rice-paper wrappers
¹/₂ small Lebanese (short) cucumber,
julienned
¹/₂ carrot, julienned
10 g (¹/₂ cup) mint
50 g (¹/₃ cup) roasted salted cashews,
roughly chopped

For the dipping sauce:
3 tbs hoisin sauce
2 tbs kecap manis
1 tbs lime juice

Vermicelli doesn't need to be cooked — simply soak it in plenty of boiling water for about 10 minutes to soften it. Drain well.

Pat the tofu dry and cut into four thick slices. Heat the sesame and peanut oils in a large frying pan and fry the tofu over high heat until golden brown on both sides, about 2 minutes each side. Drain on paper towels, then cut each slice into four widthways.

Now onto the rice-paper wrappers. They are quite delicate so treat them gently. Fill a bowl with warm water and dip one wrapper at a time into the water until pliable, which will only take 15 seconds or so.

Lay one wrapper at a time on a work surface, then top with some vermicelli, tofu, cucumber, carrot, mint and cashews. Roll tightly, folding in the sides, and place on a plate, seam-side down. The rolls can dry out quite quickly, so keep them covered with a clean, damp cloth while you roll up the rest.

Now mix together all the dipping sauce ingredients in a small bowl. Put it on a platter with the spring rolls and watch them all go. Makes 16.

pumpkin soup with sage pesto

1 kg (2 lb 4 oz) butternut pumpkin (squash), peeled, seeded and chopped
2 floury potatoes, peeled and chopped
2 large onions, chopped
1.5 litres (6 cups) good-quality vegetable stock
pinch of freshly grated nutmeg
125 ml (^{1}/2 cup) cream

For the sage pesto:
10 g (^{1}/2 cup) sage
20 g (1 cup) flat-leaf (Italian) parsley
2 garlic cloves, crushed
1 tbs pine nuts, toasted
35 g (^{1}/3 cup) walnuts, toasted
4 tbs extra virgin olive oil
^{1}/2 tsp sea salt
3 tbs freshly grated Parmesan cheese

This soup is so easy! Just put the pumpkin, potato, onion and stock in a large saucepan and bring to the boil over high heat. Reduce the heat and simmer for about half an hour until the vegetables are soft — you can test them with the point of a sharp knife.

To make the sage pesto, blitz the sage, parsley, garlic, pine nuts, walnuts, olive oil and sea salt in a food processor until smooth — or use a mortar and pestle if you want to put in a bit of muscle. Scoop the pesto into a small bowl and stir in the Parmesan. Season to taste with salt and pepper.

Let the soup cool a little, then blitz in batches in a blender until smooth. Return to the cleaned saucepan and season with the nutmeg, salt and pepper. Stir in the cream, gently reheat, and serve topped with a dollop of sage pesto.
Serves 4.

Pumpkin soup speaks of roaring fires, good friends, a bottle of wine and a board game — sage pesto is a wise accompaniment.

Nothing sings of spring like asparagus. Known in the eighteenth century as sparrow grass, these delicate green spears are far too lovely to leave for the birds.

asparagus with poached quail eggs and lime hollandaise

32 fresh asparagus spears, trimmed
2 tbs virgin olive oil
2 tsp freshly ground black pepper
2 tsp white vinegar
12 quail eggs
a sprinkling of paprika
shavings of good-quality Parmesan cheese

For the lime hollandaise:
2 free-range egg yolks
150 g (5 1/2 oz) butter, melted
2 tbs lime juice

Brush the asparagus spears with a little of the oil, then roll them around in the pepper, shaking off any excess.

Half-fill a deep frying pan with water and bring to a gentle simmer, then splash in the vinegar. Crack each quail egg into a small bowl, then gently slide them one at a time into the pan. (You will probably need to cook them in two batches.) Cook until the egg white turns opaque, about 1–2 minutes, then carefully remove from the pan with a slotted spoon and keep somewhere warm.

Heat the remaining oil in a large frying pan and cook the asparagus over high heat until tender and bright green, about 2–3 minutes.

To make the lime hollandaise, whiz the egg yolks in a blender or whisk by hand and slowly add the melted butter in a thin, steady stream. Mix until all the butter has been added and you have a thick, creamy sauce. Stir in the lime juice, season to taste with salt and black pepper, then mix well.

Divide the asparagus among four warmed serving plates, top with three quail eggs per person, drizzle with some hollandaise and sprinkle with paprika and Parmesan shavings. Serve immediately.
Serves 4.

gazpacho

For the soup:

500 g (1 lb 2 oz) ripe tomatoes
1 cucumber, chopped
1 red capsicum (pepper), chopped
1 small green capsicum (pepper), chopped
2 garlic cloves, crushed
1 small red onion, chopped
2 tbs chopped mint
1/4 tsp Tabasco
3 tbs red wine vinegar
100 ml (3 1/2 fl oz) virgin olive oil
400 g (14 oz) can chopped tomatoes
250 ml (1 cup) vegetable stock

1 tbs olive oil
2 thick slices white bread, crusts removed,
cut into 1 cm (1/2 inch) cubes
shredded mint leaves
finely diced avocado

The easiest way to peel the tomatoes is to score a cross in the base of each of them, then sit them in a bowl of boiling water for 10 seconds. Plunge into cold water and peel the skin away from the cross. Now cut the tomatoes into quarters.

Put all the soup ingredients except the canned tomatoes and stock in a food processor and blitz until roughly combined.

Scoop the mixture into a bowl, then stir in the canned tomatoes, stock and 250 ml (1 cup) water. Now refrigerate for at least 2 hours — gazpacho should be served thoroughly chilled.

For the finishing touch, make some crispy croutons. Heat the oil in a small frying pan and fry the bread cubes over medium heat until golden — they'll only need 3–5 minutes. Garnish the soup with your croutons, some mint and the diced avocado.
Serves 4–6.

This is much, much more than just a chilled tomato soup. Light, tangy and garlicky, gazpacho offers extreme refreshment on a hot summer's day — especially after a long, lazy siesta.

True salt-of-the earth peasant fare, this hearty Italian soup would once have fuelled the workers in the field from dawn to dusk, so it will easily fuel you through a day at the office. Plan ahead so you have plenty of time to soak the beans.

italian bean and barley soup

200 g (7 oz) dried borlotti beans
2 tbs olive oil
1 small onion, thinly sliced
2 garlic cloves, crushed
1.5 litres (6 cups) vegetable stock
1 tbs finely chopped thyme or sage
200 g (7 oz) pearl barley
100 g (1 cup) grated Parmesan cheese
1 tbs finely chopped parsley
4 tsp extra virgin olive oil

Soak the borlotti beans in cold water overnight. Drain, then put them in a large saucepan with plenty of fresh cold water. Bring to the boil and simmer until tender: this will take about 1 1/2 hours depending on the age of the beans — older, drier beans may take longer to soften. Drain.

Heat the olive oil in a large saucepan and gently cook the onion until soft, about 6 minutes. Season with salt and pepper, then add the garlic and briefly cook without browning. Pour in the stock, add the thyme or sage and bring to the boil.

Stir in the barley a little at a time so that the stock continues to boil, then lower the heat and simmer for 15 minutes. Now add the drained borlotti beans and simmer for another 30 minutes — the barley should be tender and the soup thick.

Purée one-third of the soup until smooth, leaving the remainder chunky to give the soup some texture. Pour the soup back into the saucepan and stir in the Parmesan and parsley. Season, then stir in enough hot water to make a spoonable consistency — try 125 ml (1/2 cup) to start with. Serve immediately, with a teaspoon of oil stirred through each bowl.
Serves 4.

roasted stuffed mushrooms

8 large mushrooms, about 11 cm
(4 1/2 inches) in diameter
60 g (3 tbs) butter
1 red onion, finely chopped
3 garlic cloves, finely chopped
1 small red capsicum (pepper), finely chopped
2 tbs chopped oregano
160 g (2 cups) fresh breadcrumbs
2 tsp grated lemon zest
65 g (2/3 cup) shredded Parmesan cheese
20 g (2/3 cup) chopped flat-leaf
(Italian) parsley
olive oil, for drizzling

Mushrooms should not be washed, but it's a good idea to wipe them down with a damp cloth. Cut off the stalks and finely chop them, then put the mushrooms cup-side up on a lightly oiled baking tray.

Now heat the butter in a large frying pan. Add the onion and garlic and cook for 2 minutes over medium heat, then add the mushroom stalks, capsicum and oregano and sauté until soft — about 5 minutes.

Take the pan off the heat, then stir in the breadcrumbs, lemon zest and Parmesan. Season with salt and pepper, and stir in most of the parsley. Pile the mixture into the mushroom cups. Drizzle with oil and bake in a 180°C (350°F/Gas 4) oven for 15 minutes, or until the mushrooms are soft and the topping is golden. Sprinkle with the rest of the parsley, and serve piping hot. Serves 4.

Don't believe everything you've heard – life is not too short to stuff a mushroom!

These fragrant, spicy bhajis are something to relish. Serve them with your favourite chutney, or rustle up a raita made from yoghurt, mint, cucumber and a squirt of lemon.

vegetable bhajis

275 g (2½ cups) besan (chickpea flour)
1 tsp chilli powder
1 tsp ground turmeric
¼ tsp asafoetida (a spice available
from Asian grocery stores)
100 g (3½ oz) carrots, julienned
100 g (3½ oz) snowpeas (mangetout),
julienned
50 g (1¾ oz) slender eggplants
(aubergines), julienned
6 curry leaves
oil, for deep-frying

In a bowl, mix together the besan and the ground spices with a pinch of salt. Add enough water to make a thick batter. Now mix all the vegetables and the curry leaves into the batter.

Fill a deep heavy-based saucepan or wok one-third full of oil and heat until a cube of bread dropped into the oil browns in 15 seconds.

Lift clumps of vegetables out of the batter and lower carefully into the oil. Fry until golden all over and cooked through, about 4 minutes, then drain on crumpled paper towels. Sprinkle with salt and serve hot with a small bowl of chutney or raita.
Makes about 20.

green pilaff with cashews

100 g (2/3 cup) cashew nuts, chopped
2 tbs olive oil
6 spring onions (scallions), chopped
300 g (1 1/2 cups) long-grain brown rice
2 garlic cloves, finely chopped
1 tsp fennel seeds
2 tbs lemon juice
625 ml (2 1/2 cups) vegetable stock
200 g (7 oz) baby English spinach, shredded
3 tbs chopped mint
3 tbs chopped flat-leaf (Italian) parsley

Scatter the cashews on a baking tray and roast in a 180°C (350°F/Gas 4) oven for 5–10 minutes, or until golden brown — watch them carefully so they don't burn.

Now heat the oil in a large frying pan and cook the spring onion over medium heat until soft, about 2 minutes. Add the rice, garlic and fennel seeds and cook, stirring well, until the rice is evenly coated, which will take a few minutes.

Increase the heat to high; add the lemon juice, stock and 1 teaspoon of salt and bring to the boil. Now reduce the heat to low, pop a lid on and let it cook for 45 minutes without lifting the lid — no peeking!

Remove from the heat and sprinkle with the spinach and herbs. Put the lid back on for another 8 minutes, then stir through the spinach and herbs. Season to taste and serve sprinkled with cashews.
Serves 6–8.

Bursting with fibre and essential nutrients, brown rice is truly one of nature's super foods. This cashew-studded pilaff tastes super too, and is bound to give you energy to burn, burn, burn...

Sandwiches have their place in every picnic basket, but celebrations call for something more. Rise to the occasion with this marvellous loaf. You'll need to cobble it together the night before — a cunning plan really, as it leaves you free to feast and loaf about.

couscous vegetable loaf

1 litre (4 cups) vegetable stock
500 g (1 lb 2 oz) instant couscous
30 g (1 oz) butter
3 tbs olive oil
2 garlic cloves, crushed
1 onion, finely chopped
1 tbs ground coriander
1 tsp ground cinnamon
1 tsp garam masala
250 g (1 punnet) cherry tomatoes, quartered
1 zucchini (courgette), diced
125 g (4¹/2 oz) can corn kernels, drained
60 g (1 cup) chopped basil, plus 8 large leaves
150 g (5¹/2 oz) sun-dried capsicums (peppers) in oil

For the dressing:
4 tbs orange juice
1 tbs lemon juice
3 tbs chopped flat-leaf (Italian) parsley
1 tsp honey
1 tsp ground cumin

In a saucepan, bring the stock to the boil. Put the couscous and butter into a bowl, pour in the hot stock and leave for 10 minutes.

Meanwhile, heat 1 tablespoon of the oil in a large frying pan and cook the garlic and onion over low heat until the onion is soft, about 5 minutes. Add the spices and cook for about a minute, or until fragrant. Remove from the pan and keep them handy.

Add the remaining oil to the pan and fry the tomatoes, zucchini and corn over high heat until the zucchini is soft, about 4 minutes.

Line a 3 litre (12 cup) loaf tin with plastic wrap, letting it overhang the sides. Arrange the basil leaves into two pretty flower shapes on the base of the tin. Drain the capsicums, reserving 2 tablespoons of the oil, then chop them. Toss them into the couscous with the onion mixture, tomato mixture and chopped basil. Mix well, and leave to cool.

Press the couscous mixture into the tin and fold the plastic wrap over the loaf. Weigh down with cans of food and refrigerate overnight.

Put all the dressing ingredients in a screw-top jar with the reserved capsicum oil and shake well. Turn out the loaf, cut it into slices and serve with the dressing.
Serves 6.

vietnamese salad

200 g (7 oz) dried rice vermicelli
10 g ($^1/_2$ cup) firmly packed torn
Vietnamese mint
15 g ($^1/_2$ cup) firmly packed coriander
(cilantro) leaves
$^1/_2$ red onion, cut into thin wedges
1 green mango, julienned
1 Lebanese (short) cucumber,
halved lengthways and thinly
sliced on the diagonal
140 g (1 cup) crushed unsalted peanuts

For the lemon grass dressing:
125 ml ($^1/_2$ cup) lime juice
1 tbs grated palm sugar
3 tbs seasoned rice vinegar
2 stems lemon grass, white part only,
finely chopped
2 red chillies, seeded and finely chopped
3 makrut (kaffir) lime leaves, shredded

This salad is simplicity plus. Put the vermicelli in a bowl and cover with boiling water for 10 minutes, or until soft. Drain, rinse under cold water and chop into short lengths.

Toss the vermicelli into a large bowl with the mint, coriander, onion, mango, cucumber and three-quarters of the nuts. Mix together well — don't be shy, use your hands!

To make the lemon grass dressing, put all the dressing ingredients into a screw-top jar and shake together well. Now toss the dressing through the salad and refrigerate for 30 minutes. Sprinkle with the remaining nuts just before serving.
Serves 4–6.

Crunchy, sweet, sour and seriously spicy, this salad will revive even the most jaded palate. Serve it when you're feeling dreary and let it lift you up where you belong.

In the fading heat of a summer's night, this chilled soup is supremely refreshing. A shot of dashi, a Japanese soup stock, adds an exquisite flavour to the broth. Cold comfort indeed!

cold soba noodles with japanese mushrooms

10 g (1/4 oz) dashi granules
2 tbs soy sauce
2 tbs mirin
2 1/2 tsp soft brown sugar
100 g (3 1/2 oz) fresh shiitake
mushrooms, sliced
150 g (5 1/2 oz) shimeji mushrooms,
pulled apart
150 g (5 1/2 oz) green beans, trimmed
and sliced into 4 cm (1 1/2 inch)
lengths on the diagonal
1 tbs vegetable oil
1/2 tsp sesame oil
1 tsp finely chopped fresh ginger
3 tbs rice vinegar
2 spring onions (scallions), thinly sliced
on the diagonal
400 g (14 oz) dried soba noodles
1 tbs sesame seeds, toasted

Dissolve the dashi in 1 litre (4 cups) hot water in a large saucepan. Add the soy sauce, mirin and 2 teaspoons of the sugar and bring to the boil. Add all the mushrooms and cook until wilted, about 3 minutes. Strain the liquid into a bowl, reserving the mushrooms. Let the broth cool a little, then cover and chill for 3 hours, or until cold.

Blanch the beans, then plunge into iced water until cold. Drain and add to the mushrooms.

In a small bowl, mix together the vegetable and sesame oil, ginger, rice vinegar and half the spring onion with the remaining sugar. Pour this over the mushroom mixture and mix it through well.

Half fill a large saucepan with water and bring to the boil. Add the soba noodles, bring the pot back to the boil and add 250 ml (1 cup) cold water. Repeat three times as the water comes to the boil. Drain the noodles and cool them under cold running water.

Divide the noodles among four serving bowls and pour in the chilled broth. Arrange the vegetables on top. Serve sprinkled with sesame seeds and the remaining spring onion.
Serves 4.

what's for dinner?

meals to match any occasion

Succulent Asian greens and crunchy snake beans are the dream team behind this satisfying stir-fry. Crispy fried onion adds extra crunch.

asian greens with teriyaki tofu dressing

4 tbs soft brown sugar
1/2 tsp ground chilli
2 tbs grated fresh ginger
250 ml (1 cup) teriyaki sauce
3 tbs oil
1 onion, thinly sliced
750 g (2 bunches) baby bok choy
(pak choi), cut into thirds
500 g (1 lb 2 oz) choy sum, cut into thirds
450 g (1 lb) snake beans, trimmed and
cut into 10 cm (4 inch) lengths
1 tbs sesame oil
600 g (1 lb 5 oz) silken firm tofu, drained

Once you start stir-frying, there's no turning back, so have everything ready before you begin. First make a stir-fry sauce by mixing together the sugar, chilli, ginger and teriyaki sauce in a small bowl. Keep it handy.

Heat a wok over high heat, add 1 tablespoon of the oil and swirl it around to coat the side of the wok. Cook the onion a little at a time until crisp, about 4 minutes. Remove with a slotted spoon and drain on paper towels.

Heat another tablespoon of the oil in the wok. Add half the Asian greens and snake beans and stir-fry briefly until the Asian greens are wilted, about 3 minutes. Scoop them out of the wok and keep them warm. Heat the rest of the oil, stir-fry the rest of the greens and beans, then scoop them out and add them to the other vegetables. Drain any liquid from the wok.

Now for the teriyaki tofu dressing. Pour your stir-fry sauce into the wok, bring to the boil, then reduce the heat and simmer for 1 minute. Add the sesame oil and tofu and simmer for 2 minutes, turning once — the tofu will break up. Now divide all the greens among serving plates, then drizzle with the teriyaki tofu dressing. Sprinkle with the crispy onion and serve with plenty of steaming jasmine rice. Serves 6.

mediterranean paella

200 g (1 cup) dried haricot beans
1/4 tsp saffron threads
2 tbs olive oil
1 onion, diced
1 red capsicum (pepper), thinly sliced
5 garlic cloves, crushed
275 g (1 1/4 cups) paella or risotto rice
1 tbs sweet paprika
1/2 tsp mixed spice
750 ml (3 cups) vegetable stock
400 g (14 oz) can chopped tomatoes
1 1/2 tbs tomato paste (purée)
150 g (1 cup) shelled fresh or frozen soya beans
100 g (3 1/2 oz) silverbeet (Swiss chard) leaves (no stems), shredded
400 g (14 oz) can artichoke hearts, drained and quartered
4 tbs chopped coriander (cilantro) leaves

Soak the haricot beans overnight in plenty of cold water. Drain and rinse them well.

Briefly dry-fry the saffron threads in a small pan over medium heat until darkened — shake the pan while cooking so they don't burn. Remove from the heat and when cool, crumble into a small bowl. Pour in 125 ml (1/2 cup) warm water and leave to steep.

Heat the oil in a large frying pan. Add the onion and capsicum and cook over medium heat until the onion softens, about 5 minutes. Stir in the garlic, cook for 1 minute, then reduce the heat and add the haricot beans, rice, paprika, mixed spice and 1/2 tsp salt. Give a good stir, then add the saffron water, stock, tomatoes and tomato paste and bring to the boil. Pop the lid on, reduce the heat and simmer for 20 minutes without stirring.

Now stir in the soya beans, silverbeet and artichoke, pop the lid back on, then cook until all the liquid is absorbed and the rice and beans are tender, about 10 minutes. Turn off the heat and leave for 5 minutes. Stir in the coriander and wait for the compliments to roll. Serves 6.

Delicate, exquisite and ambrosial, saffron threads are plucked from the stigmas of the crocus flower. A pinch is enough to make any dish really special. And this paella is definitely special — something to share with your dearest friends.

The slow, leisurely cooking of mushrooms infuses this peppery pilaff with a deeply earthy essence. Even non-vegetarians will marvel at this wonderful concoction — abundance in a bowl.

pearl barley and asian mushroom pilaff

330 g (1½ cups) pearl barley
3 dried shiitake mushrooms
500 g (1 lb 2 oz) mixed fresh mushrooms
(we used oyster, Swiss brown and enoki)
625 ml (2½ cups) good-quality
vegetable stock
125 ml (½ cup) dry sherry
2 tbs olive oil
1 large onion, finely chopped
3 garlic cloves, crushed
2 tbs grated fresh ginger
1 tsp Sichuan peppercorns, crushed
500 g (1 lb 2 oz) choy sum, cut into
short lengths
3 tsp kecap manis
1 tsp sesame oil

Soak the barley in plenty of cold water for at least 6 hours, preferably overnight. Drain.

Cover the shiitake mushrooms with boiling water and soak for 15 minutes. Meanwhile, slice the oyster and Swiss brown mushrooms, and separate the delicate enoki mushrooms. Strain the shiitake mushrooms, reserving 125 ml (½ cup) of the flavoursome liquid. Discard the stalks and thinly slice the caps.

In a small saucepan, heat the stock and sherry — keep gently bubbling until needed.

Heat the oil in a large saucepan and cook the onion over medium heat until softened, about 5 minutes. Add the garlic, ginger and peppercorns and cook briefly. Increase the heat and add the oyster and Swiss brown mushrooms. Cook until soft, about 6 minutes.

Throw in the barley, hot stock, the shiitake mushrooms and their soaking liquid. Give a good stir and bring to the boil. Now reduce the heat, pop the lid on and simmer until the liquid has evaporated, about 35 minutes.

Steam the choy sum until just wilted, about 1–2 minutes. Add to the pilaff with the enoki mushrooms, stir in the kecap manis and sesame oil and you're ready to serve. Serves 4.

roasted chunky ratatouille cannelloni

1 eggplant (aubergine)
2 zucchini (courgettes)
1 large red capsicum (pepper)
1 large green capsicum (pepper)
3–4 ripe Roma (plum) tomatoes
12 unpeeled garlic cloves
3 tbs olive oil
300 g (10 1/2 oz) can tomato passata
(puréed tomatoes)
350 g (12 oz) cannelloni tubes
3 tbs shredded basil
310 g (1 1/4 cups) ricotta cheese
100 g (3 1/2 oz) feta cheese
1 free-range egg, lightly beaten
45 g (1/2 cup) grated pecorino cheese

Cut the eggplant, zucchini, capsicums and tomatoes into 2 cm (3/4 inch) cubes and toss them all into an ovenproof dish along with the garlic cloves. Drizzle with the olive oil and toss to coat — the easiest way is to get your hands in there. Now bake in a 200°C (400°F/Gas 6) oven for 1 1/2 hours, or until the vegetables are tender and the tomatoes slightly mushy. Peel the garlic and lightly mash — it will be deliciously mild and creamy. Add it to the ratatouille mixture.

Pour the passata into a large ovenproof dish. Spoon the ratatouille into the cannelloni tubes and arrange them in the dish. Now combine the basil, ricotta and feta with the beaten egg, then season well and spoon the mixture over the cannelloni. Sprinkle with the pecorino cheese and put the whole thing back in the oven for 30 minutes, or until the cannelloni is seductively soft. Splendid served with a crisp green salad.
Serves 6–8.

If stuffing a cannelloni tube seems too fiddly or just too daunting, you could easily use fresh lasagne sheets for this recipe instead — just put a line of filling down the middle and roll them up into tubes. So you see, there's really no excuse not to try this sumptuous dish!

Stir-fried noodles offer oodles of satisfaction when you're yearning for a supper that'll make your senses sing. A few minutes of chopping, then grab a wok, fire it up, toss a few things in and soon you've got a sizzling nest of slippery noodles to slurp your way through.

hokkien noodles with asian greens and glazed tofu

3 tbs kecap manis
1 tbs mushroom soy sauce
1 tbs vegetarian oyster sauce
300 g (10½ oz) firm tofu, cut into
1 cm (½ inch) steaks
1 tsp sesame oil
3 tbs peanut oil
2 garlic cloves, crushed
1 tbs grated fresh ginger
1 onion, cut into wedges
350 g (1 bunch) choy sum, roughly chopped
375 g (1 bunch) baby bok choy (pak choi),
roughly chopped
450 g (1 lb) fresh hokkien (egg) noodles,
separated

Firstly, make a marinade by mixing together the kecap manis, soy sauce and oyster sauce. Put the tofu into a shallow, non-metallic dish, pour the marinade over and let the tofu marinate for 15 minutes (or longer if you have the time — the longer the better, really). When you're ready, drain the tofu, but don't throw away that yummy marinade.

Heat a wok over high heat, add the sesame oil and 1 tablespoon of the peanut oil and swirl around to coat the side of the wok. Add the garlic, ginger and onion and stir-fry until the onion is soft, about 2–3 minutes. Remove from the wok and keep somewhere warm. Throw the Asian greens into the wok and stir-fry for a few minutes until just wilted, then remove and add to the onion mixture.

Now toss the separated noodles and the reserved marinade into the wok and stir-fry for a few minutes until the noodles are nicely coated and heated through. Remove from the wok and swirl them into nests on four warmed serving plates.

Finally, heat the rest of the peanut oil and fry the tofu for a few minutes until browned on both sides. Arrange on top of the noodles with the greens and spicy onion mixture, then dig in without delay.
Serves 4.

tofu in black bean sauce

4 tbs vegetable stock
2 tsp cornflour (cornstarch)
2 tsp Chinese rice wine
1 tsp sesame oil
1 tbs soy sauce
2 tbs peanut oil
450 g (1 lb) firm tofu, cut into 2 cm
(3/4 inch) cubes
2 garlic cloves, very finely chopped
2 tsp finely chopped fresh ginger
3 tbs fermented black beans, rinsed
and very finely chopped
4 spring onions (scallions), cut
on the diagonal
1 red capsicum (pepper), cut into 2 cm
(3/4 inch) chunks
300 g (10 1/2 oz) baby bok choy (pak choi),
chopped crossways into 2 cm
(3/4 inch) pieces

Firstly, make a simmer sauce by mixing together the stock, cornflour, Chinese rice wine, sesame oil and soy sauce in a small bowl with 1/2 teaspoon salt and freshly ground black pepper.

Heat a wok over medium heat, add the peanut oil and swirl it around to coat the side of the wok. Add the tofu and stir-fry in two batches until lightly browned — each batch will take about 3 minutes. Remove with a slotted spoon and drain on paper towels. Discard any bits of tofu stuck to the wok or floating in the oil.

Now throw the garlic and ginger into the wok and stir-fry for 30 seconds. Toss in the black beans and spring onion and stir-fry for 30 seconds. Add the capsicum and stir-fry for 1 minute, then add the bok choy and stir-fry for a further 2 minutes. Return the tofu to the wok and stir gently.

Finally, pour in the simmer sauce and stir gently for 2–3 minutes, or until the sauce thickens slightly. Serve with lots of steamed rice to soak up the black bean sauce. Serves 4.

Black beans are actually our old friend the soya bean, fermented and preserved. Here they add a special dimension to this deliciously gingery stew — just the ticket when you're hankering for something hearty and restorative.

Purity is a cornerstone of Buddhist cuisine, which evolved in the monasteries of China and Japan. Buddhist philosophy goes far beyond vegetarianism, treating the mind, body and environment with gentle respect.

buddhist vegetarian noodles

15 g (1/2 oz) dried Chinese mushrooms
400 g (14 oz) fresh flat egg noodles
2–3 tbs peanut oil
1 small carrot, julienned
150 g (51/2 oz) fresh baby corn, sliced
into quarters lengthways
225 g (8 oz) can julienned bamboo
shoots, drained
150 g (51/2 oz) snow peas (mangetout),
julienned
1/2 small red capsicum (pepper), julienned
1 small green capsicum (pepper), julienned
90 g (31/4 oz) bean sprouts, trimmed
40 g (11/2 oz) Chinese cabbage,
finely shredded
2 x 2 cm (3/4 x 3/4 inch) piece fresh ginger,
peeled and julienned
1 tbs mushroom soy sauce
1 tbs light soy sauce
1 tbs Chinese rice wine
2 tbs vegetarian oyster sauce
1 tsp sesame oil
ground white pepper
2 tbs coriander (cilantro) leaves

Soak the Chinese mushrooms in boiling water for 20 minutes. Drain, discard the woody stems and thinly slice the caps. Meanwhile, cook the noodles in a large saucepan of boiling water for 1 minute, stirring to separate the strands. Drain. Rinse under cold running water, then drain again.

Heat a wok over high heat, add 1 tablespoon of the peanut oil and stir-fry the carrot and corn for 1–2 minutes. Add the bamboo shoots and stir-fry for another 1–2 minutes, or until just cooked but still crisp. Remove to a side dish. Reheat the wok (add more peanut oil if necessary) and stir-fry the snow peas and capsicums for 1–2 minutes, or until cooked but still crisp. Add to the carrot mixture.

Reheat the wok, adding a little more peanut oil, and stir-fry the bean sprouts, cabbage and mushrooms for 30 seconds. Now add the ginger and stir-fry for 1–2 minutes. Remove and add to the other vegetables.

Heat the remaining peanut oil in the wok, then gently stir-fry the noodles until heated through. Stir in the soy sauces, rice wine and oyster sauce, then add all the vegetables, stirring gently for a few minutes. Drizzle with the sesame oil, season with white pepper, sprinkle with coriander and serve. Serves 4.

green curry with sweet potato and eggplant

1 tbs oil
1 onion, chopped
1–2 tbs green curry paste (check the label,
as some curry pastes contain shrimp paste)
1 eggplant (aubergine), quartered and sliced
375 ml (1 1/2 cups) coconut milk
250 ml (1 cup) vegetable stock
6 makrut (kaffir) lime leaves, plus a few extra
1 orange sweet potato, peeled and
cut into cubes
2 tsp soft brown sugar
2 tbs lime juice
2 tsp finely grated lime zest
coriander (cilantro) leaves

Heat the oil in a large wok or frying pan and swirl to coat the side of the wok. Add the onion and green curry paste and stir over medium heat until it smells fabulously spicy, about 3 minutes. Add the eggplant and cook until softened, about 4–5 minutes.

Pour in the coconut milk and vegetable stock. Bring to the boil, then reduce the heat and simmer for 5 minutes. Add the lime leaves and sweet potato and cook for about 10 minutes, stirring now and then — the eggplant and sweet potato should become very tender.

Now splash in the sugar, lime juice and lime zest, mixing them in well. Check if the curry needs a little salt, then scatter with some coriander and lime leaves. Serve with buckets of steamed jasmine rice.
Serves 4–6.

The magical thing about curries is that the longer you leave them, the better they become. Make this popular curry the day before you intend to eat it — or better still, why not make extra so you can dine out on seconds and thirds during the week?

In Japan, tofu is taken seriously indeed. Well before the crack of dawn, specialist tofu shops start churning out fresh batches daily for discerning customers. Sadly, we'll have to make do with the packet variety, but when it's in a burger as stupendous as this, it's nothing to lose sleep over.

tofu burgers

For the burgers:
1 tbs olive oil
1 red onion, finely chopped
200 g (7 oz) Swiss brown mushrooms, finely chopped
350 g (12 oz) firm tofu
2 large garlic cloves
3 tbs finely chopped basil
350 g (3 1/2 cups) dry wholemeal breadcrumbs
1 free-range egg, lightly beaten
2 tbs balsamic vinegar
2 tbs sweet chilli sauce, plus a little extra

olive oil, for pan-frying
6 wholemeal or wholegrain bread rolls
125 g (1 1/2 cup) whole-egg mayonnaise
100 g (3 1/2 oz) semi-dried (sun-blushed) tomatoes
60 g (2 1/4 oz) rocket (arugula)

Heat the oil in a frying pan and cook the onion over medium heat for 5 minutes, or until soft. Add the mushrooms and cook for another 2 minutes. Leave to cool slightly.

To make the burgers, put 250 g (9 oz) of the tofu into a food processor with the garlic and basil and blitz until smooth. Scrape it into a large bowl, then stir in the mushroom mixture, (200 g) 2 cups of the breadcrumbs, the egg, vinegar and sweet chilli sauce. Grate the remaining tofu, stir it through, then refrigerate for 30 minutes. Now divide the mixture into six portions, then shape into pretty patties, pressing them together firmly. Smother them in the rest of the breadcrumbs.

Heat about 1 cm (1/2 inch) of oil in a deep frying pan. Cook the burgers in two batches over medium heat for 4–5 minutes on each side, until golden — flip them over gently as they may be fragile. Drain on crumpled paper towels and season with salt. Meanwhile, toast the bread rolls under a hot grill (broiler).

To assemble, spread a dollop of mayonnaise over the inside halves of each toasted roll. Put some semi-dried tomatoes on the bottom half, then a patty and some rocket leaves. Drizzle with sweet chilli sauce and top with the other half roll. Start munching, mmm… Serves 6.

somen nests with eggplant and shiitake mushrooms

2 small eggplants (aubergines), cut into
1 cm (1/2 inch) slices
12 dried shiitake mushrooms
3 tbs vegetable oil
100 g (3 1/2 oz) fresh enoki mushrooms
325 g (11 1/2 oz) dried somen noodles

For the simmer sauce:
1 tsp dashi granules
1 tbs sugar
1 tbs white miso paste
1 tbs mirin
3 tbs Japanese soy sauce

Blanch the eggplant slices in 250 ml (1 cup) boiling water for 5 minutes. Drain the eggplant, put it on a plate and weigh it down with another plate for 15 minutes to squish out any remaining liquid. Pat dry.

Soak the shiitake mushrooms in some boiling water for 15 minutes. Drain the liquid, but don't throw it away. Heat the oil in a large frying pan and cook the eggplant slices in batches over medium heat until golden brown on both sides, about 2–3 minutes each side. Remove and keep warm. Toss the enoki mushrooms in the wok and cook for a mere 10 seconds. Remove.

Now add the simmer sauce ingredients to the wok, along with the shiitake mushrooms, their soaking liquid and 125 ml (1/2 cup) water. Bring to the boil, then reduce the heat, pop a lid on and simmer for 10 minutes.

Meanwhile, cook the noodles in boiling water until tender, about 3 minutes. Drain, then divide the noodles among four serving plates, swirling them into nests to hold the eggplant slices and mushrooms. Drizzle with the simmer sauce and enjoy without delay. Serves 4.

Japanese somen noodles are made by stretching dough out over several months and daubing it with vegetable oil to stop it drying out. Thankfully, you don't need to go to such exorbitant lengths to enjoy this dish, which takes very little effort to heat and eat.

Melt-in-the-mouth onions make a memorable meal of these sprightly patties. Scoff them down with a salad, or make a hunger-busting burger out of them.

chickpea patties with caramelized onion

1 tbs olive oil
1 red onion, finely chopped
2 garlic cloves, crushed
1 tbs ground cumin
2 x 300 g (10½ oz) cans chickpeas, drained
3 tbs sunflower seeds
25 g (½ cup) finely chopped coriander
(cilantro) leaves
2 free-range eggs, lightly beaten
75 g (⅔ cup) besan (chickpea flour)
oil, for pan-frying
Greek-style yoghurt

For the caramelized onion:
40 g (1½ oz) butter
2 red onions, thinly sliced
3 tsp soft brown sugar

Heat the oil in a frying pan, add the onion and cook over medium heat until soft, about 5 minutes. Add the garlic and cumin, cook for about a minute, then remove from the heat and let the mixture cool slightly.

Now put the onion mixture into a food processor with the chickpeas, sunflower seeds, coriander and egg, and blitz until smooth. Scoop the mixture into a bowl, then fold in the besan and season well. Divide the mixture into eight portions and, using floured hands, shape them into lovely patties.

Heat about 1 cm (½ inch) oil in a frying pan and cook the patties in two batches over medium heat for 2–3 minutes each side, or until firm. Drain on paper towels and keep warm.

Meanwhile, you may as well caramelize those onions. Simply melt the butter in a small frying pan over medium heat and cook the onion for 10 minutes, stirring now and then. Add the sugar and cook for another minute, or until the onions are sweetly caramelized.

Now spoon the onions over the patties, along with a good dollop of yoghurt. Serve with a green salad while nice and hot. Serves 4.

roast sweet potato ravioli

500 g (1 lb 2 oz) orange sweet potato, peeled and cut into large pieces
3 tbs olive oil
150 g (5 1/2 oz) ricotta cheese
1 tbs chopped basil
3 garlic cloves, crushed
2 tbs grated Parmesan cheese
2 x 250 g (9 oz) packets egg won ton wrappers
50 g (1 3/4 oz) butter
4 spring onions (scallions), sliced on the diagonal
300 ml (10 1/2 fl oz) cream
torn basil leaves

Put the sweet potato on a baking tray and drizzle with oil. Bake in a 220°C (425°F/ Gas 7) oven for 40 minutes, or until tender. Transfer the sweet potato to a bowl with the ricotta, basil, a third of the garlic and all the Parmesan, and mash together until smooth.

Take the won ton wrappers from their packets and cover with a damp tea towel. Spoon 2 level teaspoons of the filling into the centre of a wrapper. Brush the edges with water, top with another wrapper and gently squish the edges together. Place on a baking tray lined with baking paper, and cover with a tea towel. Now keep going until you have 60 ravioli — your efforts will be rewarded!

Melt the butter in a frying pan, add the spring onion and remaing garlic; cook over medium heat for 1 minute. Add the cream, bring to the boil, then reduce the heat and simmer for 4–5 minutes, or until the cream has reduced and thickened. Keep warm.

Bring a large pot of salted water to the boil. Cook the ravioli in batches until tender, about 2–4 minutes. Drain, divide among serving plates, top with lashings of creamy sauce, scatter with basil and serve to six lucky souls. Serves 6.

Soft, creamy sweet potato makes a delectable filling for this ravishing ravioli. For a lighter meal you could serve the ravioli in a shallow dish of clear vegetable broth, with a sprinkling of spring onion.

Tough day, late night, no time? Twenty minutes in the kitchen is all it takes to orchestrate this easy classic. Pour yourself a glass of red to sip on while you cook, then kick back with a big bowl of this pasta and you'll be singing like Pavarotti.

pasta with fresh tomato and basil sauce

6 large vine-ripened tomatoes
500 g (1 lb 2 oz) penne rigate pasta
4 tbs extra virgin olive oil
4 garlic cloves, crushed
2 small red chillies, seeded and
finely chopped
4 tbs white wine
1 tbs tomato paste (purée)
2 tsp sugar
2 tbs finely chopped flat-leaf (Italian) parsley
3 tbs shredded basil
freshly grated Parmesan cheese

The easiest way to peel the tomatoes is to score a cross in the base of each of them, then sit them in a bowl of boiling water for 10 seconds. Plunge into cold water and peel the skin away from the cross. Now remove the seeds and dice the tomatoes.

Cook the pasta in a large pot of boiling salted water until *al dente*. Drain well.

Meanwhile, heat the oil in a frying pan, add the garlic and cook over medium heat for just 30 seconds. Stir in the chilli, then fry for a further 30 seconds. Now turn the heat up high, throw in the tomatoes and cook for 2 minutes. Slosh in the wine, tomato paste and sugar, pop the lid on, then reduce the heat and simmer for 10 minutes, or until nicely thickened.

Toss the tomato sauce through the pasta with the fresh herbs. Season and serve with freshly grated Parmesan. Heaven.
Serves 4.

roast vegetable tart

2 slender eggplants (aubergines),
halved and cut into thick slices
350 g (12 oz) pumpkin, peeled and cut
into large pieces
2 zucchini (courgettes), halved and cut
into thick slices
1–2 tbs olive oil
1 large red capsicum (pepper), chopped
1 tsp olive oil, extra
1 red onion, cut into thin wedges
1 tbs korma curry paste
Greek-style yoghurt

For the pastry:
185 g (1¹/2 cups) plain (all-purpose) flour
125 g (4¹/2 oz) butter, chopped
100 g (²/3 cup) roasted cashews,
finely chopped
1 tsp cumin seeds
2–3 tbs chilled water

Put the eggplant, pumpkin and zucchini on a lined baking tray, brush with oil and bake for 30 minutes in a 200°C (400°F/Gas 6) oven. Turn the vegetables over, add the capsicum and bake for 30 minutes more. Remove and turn the oven down to 180°C (350°F/Gas 4).

Meanwhile, heat the extra oil in a frying pan and cook the onion over medium heat until soft, about 5 minutes. Add the curry paste and stir for 1 minute. Take it off the hob.

To make the pastry, sift the flour into a large bowl. Rub the butter into the flour with your fingertips until it resembles fine breadcrumbs. Stir in the cashews and cumin seeds, make a well in the centre and add the water. Using a cutting action, mix with a flat-bladed knife until the mixture comes together in beads. Gather the dough together, lift onto a sheet of baking paper, flatten to a disc, then roll out to a circle 35 cm (14 inches) in diameter.

Lift the pastry onto a baking tray. Spread the onion mixture over the top, leaving a 6 cm (2¹/2 inch) border. Arrange the vegetables over the onion, piling them slightly higher in the centre. Working your way around, fold the pastry edges in pleats over the filling, then bake for 45 minutes, until the pastry is golden. Serve hot or cold with the yoghurt. Serves 4–6.

This is a tart to lift the heart with its vibrant colours and crunchy, nutty base. It makes a light, elegant lunch and fits neatly into our old friend the picnic basket.

Almost a one-pot wonder, this creamy risotto makes a lovely supper with its decadent scattering of pistachios. Stirring the risotto can be a pleasurable pastime when you have a buddy at your side and a glass of white wine at hand.

asparagus and pistachio risotto

1 litre (4 cups) good-quality vegetable stock
250 ml (1 cup) white wine
4 tbs extra virgin olive oil
1 red onion, finely chopped
440 g (2 cups) risotto rice
2 bunches fresh asparagus spears, cut
into 3 cm (1¼ inch) pieces
125 ml (½ cup) cream
100 g (1 cup) grated Parmesan cheese
80 g (½ cup) shelled pistachios, toasted
and roughly chopped

Pour the stock and wine into a large saucepan and bring to the boil. Reduce the heat, pop the lid on and keep at a low simmer.

In another large saucepan, heat the oil. Add the onion and cook over medium heat until soft, about 5 minutes. Add the rice and stir for 1 minute, or until the rice is translucent.

Now add a ladleful of hot stock, stirring constantly over medium heat until the liquid is absorbed. Add another ladleful, and keep stirring until the stock has been absorbed. Continue in this fashion until all the stock has been absorbed and the rice is tender and creamy in texture — this will take about 20–25 minutes. During the last 5 minutes of cooking, throw in the asparagus.

Now take the pot off the heat and let the risotto stand for 2 minutes. Stir in the cream and Parmesan. Season to taste, sprinkle with pistachios and enjoy without delay.
Serves 4–6.

mighty vegie stir-fry

2 tbs oil
4 spring onions (scallions), cut into 3 cm
(1¼ inch) lengths
3 garlic cloves, crushed
1 red chilli, seeded and sliced
70 g (2½ oz) button mushrooms, quartered
100 g (3½ oz) wom bok (Chinese cabbage),
roughly chopped
2 tbs soy sauce
1 tbs vegetarian oyster sauce
3 tbs stock
½ tsp grated palm sugar
150 g (5½ oz) snow peas (mangetout)
150 g (5½ oz) cauliflower, cut into
small florets
150 g (5½ oz) broccoli, cut into small florets
chopped coriander (cilantro) leaves

Heat a wok until very hot, add the oil and swirl it around to coat the side of the wok. Toss in the spring onion, garlic and chilli and stir-fry over high heat for a mere 20 seconds. Add the mushrooms and cabbage and stir-fry for 1 minute.

Now stir in the soy sauce, oyster sauce, stock and palm sugar, then toss in the remaining vegetables. Cook for 2 minutes, or until the vegetables are tender, yet still crisp. Sprinkle with coriander and serve with plenty of steamed jasmine rice. Serves 4.

Why settle for a greasy, gluggy take-away when it only takes a second to sizzle up a stir-fry at home? The beauty of stir-fries is that you can throw in whatever vegies you happen to have — just adjust the cooking times so everything stays crunchy.

This is a simple dish to comfort and inspire. Tender, slender eggplants are infused with an intriguing smokiness from dried red chillies, brightened with herbaceous notes of lime and coriander and just enough peppercorns to give the palate a nip.

eggplant with tempeh

2 small dried red chillies
8 black peppercorns
2 garlic cloves
2 tbs chopped coriander (cilantro)
stems and leaves
4 tbs oil
100 g (3½ oz) tempeh, thinly sliced
250 g (9 oz) slender eggplants (aubergines),
cut into 2 cm (¾ inch) chunks
1 tbs soy sauce
1 tsp grated palm sugar
1 tbs lime juice

Soak the chillies in a bowl of boiling water for 15 minutes. Drain, remove the seeds and finely chop the chillies.

Put the peppercorns, garlic and coriander in a food processor and blitz into a smooth paste — add a little water if needed. You could use a mortar and pestle if you're feeling at all energetic!

Heat a wok over high heat, add the oil and swirl it around to coat the side of the wok. Add the peppercorn paste and dried chilli and stir constantly for 10 seconds. Add the tempeh and stir-fry until the tempeh is golden brown, about 2 minutes. Remove the tempeh from the wok.

Now toss the eggplant into the wok and stir-fry until golden brown, about 6 minutes. Throw the tempeh back in along with all the remaining ingredients and stir for another half a minute to heat through. Absolutely delicious served with rice.
Serves 6.

fried rice with thai basil

2 tbs oil
3 red Asian shallots, sliced
1 garlic clove, finely chopped
1 small red chilli, finely chopped
100 g (3½ oz) snake or green beans, trimmed
and cut into 3 cm (1¼ inch) lengths
1 small red capsicum (pepper), thinly sliced
90 g (3¼ oz) button mushrooms, halved
465 g (2½ cups) cooked jasmine rice
1 tsp grated palm sugar or soft brown sugar
3 tbs light soy sauce
3 tbs Thai basil, shredded, plus
a few extra leaves
1 tbs coriander (cilantro) leaves, chopped
crisp fried shallots (you can buy these in a
packet from Asian grocery stores)

Heat a wok over high heat, add the oil and swirl it around to coat the side of the wok. Toss in the shallots, garlic and chilli and stir-fry until the shallots start to brown, about 3 minutes.

Add the beans, capsicum and mushrooms, and stir-fry until the beans are tender but still a little crisp, about 3 minutes. Now stir in the rice and let it heat through.

Dissolve the palm sugar in the soy sauce, then splash it over the rice. Stir in the Thai basil and coriander, scatter with the crisp fried shallots and a few extra basil leaves — and hey presto, you're ready to eat.
Serves 4.

When you peer in the fridge and rummage through the pantry only to find a little bit of everything and not a lot of anything, fried rice saves the day. For a more substantial meal, throw in some firm tofu or roasted chopped peanuts.

Savoury and richly fragrant, this spicy curry makes a fabulous banquet centrepiece. Sambal oelek, a raw chilli paste, adds a deep, fiery heat. You'll find it in Asian grocery stores, along with candlenuts, which should never be eaten raw.

indonesian pumpkin and spinach curry

For the curry paste:
3 candlenuts
1 tbs raw peanuts
2 red Asian shallots
2 garlic cloves
2–3 tsp sambal oelek
1/4 tsp ground turmeric
1 tsp grated fresh galangal

2 tbs vegetable oil
1 onion, finely chopped
600 g (1 lb 5 oz) butternut pumpkin (squash),
peeled and cut into 2 cm (3/4 inch) cubes
250 ml (1 cup) vegetable stock
350 g (12 oz) English spinach, roughly chopped
400 ml (14 fl oz) can coconut cream
1/4 tsp sugar

First, make the curry paste: just put all the ingredients in a food processor or blender and blitz into a smooth paste.

Heat a wok over high heat, add the oil and swirl it around to coat the side of the wok. Add the curry paste and stir over low heat until fragrant, about 3–5 minutes. Add the onion and cook for 5 minutes.

Now add the pumpkin and half the stock. Pop a lid on and cook for 10 minutes, or until the pumpkin is almost cooked through. Pour in a little more of the stock, if you think it needs it.

Add the spinach, coconut cream and sugar, and season with salt. Bring to the boil, stirring constantly, then reduce the heat and simmer for 3–5 minutes, or until the spinach is cooked and the sauce has thickened slightly. Serve with plenty of steamed rice to soak up all those lovely juices.
Serves 4.

balsamic capsicum on angel hair

2 red capsicums (peppers)
2 yellow capsicums (peppers)
2 green capsicums (peppers)
4 garlic cloves, crushed
2 tbs orange juice
4 tbs balsamic vinegar
300 g (10^1/$_2$ oz) angel hair pasta
100 g (3^1/$_2$ oz) goat's cheese, crumbled
15 g (^{1}/$_2$ cup) basil leaves

Cut the capsicums into large flat pieces and place under a hot grill (broiler) until the skins blister and blacken. Leave to cool in a plastic bag, then peel away the skin and cut the flesh into thin strips.

Swish together the garlic, orange juice and balsamic vinegar in a bowl and add the roasted capsicum strips, swirling them around a bit so they're nicely coated.

Meanwhile, cook the pasta in a large pot of boiling salted water until *al dente*, then drain.

Divide the pasta among four plates. Arrange the capsicums on top, scatter with the goat's cheese and basil, and sprinkle with cracked black pepper. Serve up for four lucky souls. Serves 4.

Angel hair pasta is divine any time, but adding the slippery sweetness of roasted capsicum, the creamy tang of goat's cheese and a piquant splash of balsamic vinegar makes it devilishly good. Fortify yourself with a great goblet of golden wine and pair it with a peppery rocket salad.

Creamy, cheesy, hot and molten is the only way to go when the dark comes early and it's been cold all day. Gooey and rich, this is stuff that really sticks to the sides, and is everything midwinter's dreams are made of.

gnocchi three-cheese bake

500 g (1 lb 2 oz) fresh gnocchi
150 g (5$\frac{1}{2}$ oz) blue cheese
300 ml (10$\frac{1}{2}$ fl oz) cream
50 g (1$\frac{3}{4}$ oz) fontina cheese, thinly sliced
50 g (1$\frac{3}{4}$ oz) provolone cheese, thinly sliced

Cook the gnocchi in a large pan of boiling salted water for about 2 minutes, or until they float to the surface. Remove and drain well, then spoon into six individual ovenproof dishes.

Meanwhile, take a frying pan and heat the blue cheese and cream over low heat until combined, then simmer until the sauce thickens enough to coat the back of a spoon. Try not to lick it!

Pour the blue cheese sauce over the gnocchi, then lay the cheese slices over the top. Cook under a hot grill (broiler) until golden brown, about 3–4 minutes. Serve bubbling hot. Serves 4.

roasted vegetable pasta torte

4 small Roma (plum) tomatoes
300 g (10½ oz) orange sweet potatoes, peeled and cut into large chunks
1 red capsicum (pepper)
3 tbs oil
200 g (7 oz) fettucine
6 free-range eggs
250 ml (1 cup) milk
125 g (1 cup) grated Cheddar cheese
10 g (½ cup) flat-leaf (Italian) parsley
200 g (7 oz) feta cheese, cut into large cubes

Put the tomatoes, sweet potato and capsicum in an ovenproof dish, drizzle with the oil and season well. Bake in a 200°C (400°F/Gas 6) oven for 40 minutes, or until the vegetables are tender. Peel the capsicum and cut into large chunks.

Meanwhile, cook the pasta in a large pot of boiling salted water until *al dente*. Drain well.

Crack the eggs into a bowl. Beat them lightly, then mix in the milk and Cheddar.

Arrange half the roasted vegetables and half the parsley in a deep, greased 24 cm (10 inch) non-stick frying pan. Spread half the pasta and feta over the top, then layer with the remaining vegetables, parsley, pasta and feta. Pour the egg mixture over the top, then cook over medium low heat for 15–20 minutes, or until the torte is just set — gently lift up the edges every now and then to check the base isn't burning.

Now put the pan under a hot grill (broiler) for 6–8 minutes, so the top becomes an appetizing shade of golden brown. Leave for 5 minutes before turning out to serve. Serves 6–8.

This is an excellent dish to pull out of your hat when friends drop round for a drink or two and something hot to eat. Most of it you can prepare ahead, leaving you free to enter the fray, not banished to the kitchen cursing over a hot stove.

Derived from the word balm, balsamic means 'health giving'. Although we make no claims for its restorative properties, it certainly works some magic through this marvellous salad.

warm pasta salad

750 g (1 lb 10 oz) orange sweet potato, peeled and cut into bite-sized pieces
2 tbs extra virgin olive oil
500 g (1 lb 2 oz) farfalle pasta
325 g (11½ oz) marinated feta cheese in oil
3 tbs balsamic vinegar
155 g (1 bunch) fresh asparagus spears, cut into short lengths
100 g (3½ oz) baby rocket (arugula) or baby English spinach
2 vine-ripened tomatoes, chopped
3 tbs pine nuts, toasted

Put the sweet potato in a roasting tin, drizzle with the olive oil and season generously with sea salt and cracked black pepper. Bake in a 200°C (400°F/Gas 6) oven for 20 minutes, or until the sweet potato is tender.

Meanwhile, cook the pasta in a large pot of boiling salted water until *al dente*. Drain well.

Drain 3 tablespoons of the oil from the marinated feta and whisk it with the balsamic vinegar to make a dressing.

Steam or microwave the asparagus for a few minutes until bright green and tender. Drain well, then toss into a bowl with the pasta, sweet potato, feta, rocket, tomatoes and pine nuts. Drizzle the dressing over and gently toss through. Sprinkle with cracked black pepper and serve.
Serves 4.

artichoke risoni

30 g (1 oz) butter
1 tbs olive oil
2 fennel bulbs, sliced
350 g (12 oz) marinated artichoke hearts, drained and chopped
300 ml (10$^1/_2$ fl oz) cream
1 tbs Dijon mustard
3 tbs dry white wine
50 g ($^1/_2$ cup) grated Parmesan cheese
375 g (13 oz) risoni
80 g (2 cups) shredded English spinach

Heat the butter and olive oil in a frying pan and cook the fennel slices over medium heat until caramelized, about 20 minutes. Add the artichoke hearts and cook for another 5–10 minutes.

Add the cream, mustard, wine and Parmesan and bring to the boil. Now reduce the heat and simmer for 5 minutes, so you end up with an appetizing sauce.

Meanwhile, cook the risoni in a large pot of boiling salted water until *al dente*, then drain well. Now stir the risoni into the cream and wine sauce, then toss in the spinach and give it a good stir until the spinach has just wilted. Serve without delay. Serves 4.

When you can't decide between pasta and risotto, there's always risoni — a rice-shaped pasta that offers the convenience of the former and the comfort of the latter. Fennel and artichoke make it a peasant's feast.

This is up there with the best when it comes to no-fuss, fun-filled fare — great after a long day out in the wilds or in the office, or for marathon video nights with a gaggle of friends. Come and get it!

bean enchiladas

1 tbs light olive oil
1 onion, thinly sliced
3 garlic cloves, crushed
1 bird's eye chilli, finely chopped
2 tsp ground cumin
125 ml (1/2 cup) vegetable stock
3 tomatoes, peeled, seeded and chopped
1 tbs tomato paste (purée)
2 x 425 g (15 oz) cans three-bean mix, drained and rinsed
2 tbs chopped coriander (cilantro)
8 flour tortillas
1 small avocado, chopped
125 g (1/2 cup) light sour cream
115 g (2 cups) shredded lettuce

Heat the oil in a deep frying pan over medium heat. Throw in the onion and cook for 5 minutes, or until just soft. Add the garlic and chilli and cook for a further 30 seconds. Now add the cumin, stock, tomato and tomato paste and cook for 6–8 minutes, or until the mixture is quite thick and pulpy. Season with salt and freshly ground black pepper.

Mix the beans into the sauce and cook for 5 minutes to heat through, then stir in the chopped coriander.

Meanwhile, warm the tortillas by wrapping them in foil and putting them in a 170°C (325°F/Gas 3) oven for a few minutes.

Put the tortillas, avocado, sour cream, lettuce and bean sauce on a large platter and let everyone assemble their own tortillas. How easy is that!
Serves 4.

conchiglie stuffed with roast pumpkin and ricotta

1 kg (2 lb 4 oz) butternut pumpkin (squash),
peeled and cut into large wedges
olive oil, for drizzling
10 unpeeled garlic cloves
500 g (2 cups) ricotta cheese
4 tbs finely shredded basil
750 ml (3 cups) pomodoro (bottled Italian
pasta sauce)
125 ml ($\frac{1}{2}$ cup) dry white wine
56 conchiglie pasta shells (or
32 giant conchiglie)
100 g (1 cup) grated Parmesan cheese

Place the pumpkin in a roasting tin, drizzle with olive oil and season well. Bake for 30 minutes in a 200°C (400°F/Gas 6) oven, then throw in the garlic cloves and bake for another 20 minutes, or until everything is tender. Leave to cool a little, then peel the pumpkin and the garlic and mash them together. Now mix in the ricotta and half the basil and season to taste.

Pour the pasta sauce and wine into a pan, stir well and bring to the boil. Reduce the heat and let it simmer for 10 minutes, or until slightly thickened.

Meanwhile, cook the pasta in a large pot of boiling salted water until *al dente*. Drain well, and when cool enough to handle, lay the shells out on a tea towel to dry.

Now spoon the pumpkin mixture into each pasta shell. If you have any filling left over, spread it over the base of a large ovenproof dish, then put the pasta shells on top. Pour over the pomodoro sauce, then sprinkle with the Parmesan and the rest of the basil. Bake the smaller shells for 15–20 minutes — the giant shells will need about 30 minutes. Serves 6.

Some suppers offer a rich, savoury experience and this is one of them. Roasted garlic gives such an enticingly sweet, smoky character to this dish that you might end up just as stuffed as the conchiglie!

Preserved lemons add a real wow factor to this heady, spicy, fruity stew. The word tagine refers to the earthenware vessel with a distinctive pointed lid traditionally used to cook this dish, as well as the meal itself. For simplicity's sake, we'll just cook it in the oven.

vegetable tagine with orange-infused couscous

1 tbs oil
2 onions, chopped
1 tsp ground ginger
2 tsp paprika
2 tsp ground cumin
1 cinnamon stick
pinch of saffron threads
1.5 kg (3 lb 5 oz) vegetables — try carrot, eggplant (aubergine), peeled potato and peeled pumpkin, cut into large chunks
half a preserved lemon, rinsed
400 g (14 oz) can tomatoes
250 ml (1 cup) vegetable stock
100 g (3½ oz) dried pears, halved
50 g (1¾ oz) pitted prunes
2 zucchini (courgettes), cut into large chunks
300 g (10½ oz) instant couscous
1 tsp grated orange zest
3 tbs chopped flat-leaf (Italian) parsley

Take a large, flameproof casserole dish and pop it on the stovetop. Heat the oil, add the onion and spices, and cook over medium heat until nice and soft, about 8 minutes.

Add all the vegetables (except the zucchini) and cook until soft — this will probably take about 15 minutes, depending on what sort you actually put in the pot.

Scrape the flesh from the preserved lemon — it is too bitter to eat! Rinse the peel, thinly slice it and throw it into your dish with the tomatoes, stock, pears and prunes. Cover and bake in a 180°C (350°F/Gas 4) oven for 30 minutes, then add the zucchini and cook for 15 minutes, or until all the vegetables are tender. Stir in the parsley and keep warm.

Cover the couscous with 500 ml (2 cups) boiling water, stir in the orange zest and find something else to do for the next 5 minutes while all the water is being absorbed. Fluff up the couscous with a fork, and serve with a generous helping of the vegetables. Serves 4–6.

chilli beans with polenta wedges

For the polenta wedges:
425 g (15 oz) can creamed corn
375 ml (1½ cups) vegetable stock
75 g (½ cup) instant polenta
300 g (10½ oz) can corn kernels, drained
4 tbs grated vintage Cheddar cheese
1 tbs chopped coriander (cilantro) leaves

For the chilli beans:
1 tbs olive oil
1 red onion, sliced
2 garlic cloves, crushed
1 tsp chilli powder
1 tsp paprika
1 tbs ground cumin
1 tsp ground coriander
400 g (14 oz) can kidney beans,
rinsed and drained
400 g (14 oz) can borlotti beans,
rinsed and drained
800 g (1 lb 12 oz) can tomatoes
2 tbs tomato paste (purée)
2 tbs chopped coriander (cilantro) leaves

Let's start with the polenta. Put the creamed corn and stock in a saucepan and bring to the boil. Stir in the polenta and corn kernels, and keep stirring over medium heat until the whole gluggy, gooey concoction comes away from the sides. Stir in the cheese and coriander, then pour into a 20 cm (8 inch) round cake tin lined with plastic wrap. Let the polenta cool a little until it is firm enough to cut into wedges.

Meanwhile, get cracking on the chilli beans. Heat the oil in a large saucepan, then add the onion, garlic and spices and cook over medium heat until soft, about 5 minutes. Stir in all the beans, tomatoes and tomato paste. Let it bubble away gently for 20 minutes, then stir in the coriander. Serve hot with polenta wedges.
Serves 6.

This dish should really be called Scrummy Polenta Wedges with Yummy Chilli Beans. Make an extra batch of the wedges and enjoy them toasted with lashings of butter and Parmesan whenever a snack attack seems imminent.

The mysterious, earthy flavour of porcini mushrooms makes this creamy risotto an unearthly delight. The problem is, porcini are so bewitching that once you get the taste for them, you may never be satisfied with button mushrooms again.

porcini risotto

30 g (1 oz) dried porcini mushrooms
1 litre (4 cups) good-quality vegetable stock
100 g (3½ oz) butter
1 onion, finely chopped
250 g (9 oz) fresh mushrooms, sliced
2 garlic cloves, crushed
385 g (1¾ cups) risotto rice
pinch of freshly grated nutmeg
1 tbs finely chopped parsley
50 g (½ cup) grated Parmesan cheese

Put the porcini in a bowl, cover with 500 ml (2 cups) hot water and leave to soak for 20 minutes. Squeeze the porcini dry, but keep the soaking liquid. If the porcini are large, roughly chop them. Now strain the mushroom liquid into a saucepan and add enough stock to make up to 1 litre (4 cups). Heat it up and maintain at a low simmer.

Melt the butter in a heavy-based saucepan, and cook the onion over medium heat until soft but not browned, about 5 minutes. Add the fresh mushrooms and porcini and fry for a few more minutes. Add the garlic, stir briefly, then add the rice. Stir until all the grains of rice are coated in the butter and become translucent.

Now add a ladleful of the stock. Cook at a fast simmer, stirring constantly. When the stock has been absorbed, stir in another ladleful. Continue in this fashion until all the stock has been absorbed and the rice is tender but still has a bit of bite — this will take about 20–25 minutes. Add a little more stock or water if you need to — every risotto will use a different amount.

Finally, stir in the nutmeg, parsley and half the Parmesan, season to taste, then serve sprinkled with the rest of the Parmesan. Serves 4.

eggplant parmigiana

1.5 kg (3 lb 5 oz) eggplants (aubergines),
cut into slices 2 cm (3/4 inch) thick
plain (all-purpose) flour, seasoned with
salt and pepper
350 ml (12 fl oz) olive oil
500 g (2 cups) tomato passata (puréed tomatoes)
2 tbs roughly torn basil
260 g (1 3/4 cups) chopped fresh mozzarella cheese
100 g (1 cup) grated Parmesan cheese

First, sprinkle the eggplant slices with salt and let them drain in a colander for an hour. Rinse well, then pat the slices dry on both sides with paper towels. Now coat them lightly with the flour.

Heat 125 ml (1/2 cup) of the olive oil in a large frying pan. Quickly fry the eggplant slices in batches over high heat until crisp and golden on both sides. Add more olive oil as needed and drain on paper towels as you remove each batch from the pan.

Now arrange some eggplant slices in a greased shallow 2.5 litre (10 cup) ovenproof dish, overlapping them slightly. Sprinkle with pepper and a little salt. Spoon 4 tablespoons of passata over the eggplant and scatter some basil over the top. Sprinkle with some mozzarella, followed by some Parmesan. Continue layering your masterpiece until you have used up all the ingredients, then scatter the cheeses over the top.

Now pop it into a 180°C (350°F/Gas 4) oven and bake for 30 minutes. Remove from the oven and allow to cool for 30 minutes, then enjoy with a fresh green salad.
Serves 8.

Silky, milky mozzarella is the perfect cheese to cook with. Admittedly, it is hard to eat with any pretence at elegance when the molten strings stretch out as far as the arm will reach — but when a dish tastes this good, does it really matter?

This dish takes its cue from Mediterranean climes and is one to leave bubbling away in the oven as you go about your daily chores. Before too long, it will infuse the whole house with a wildly appetizing aroma.

potato and zucchini casserole

this quorva.

3 tbs olive oil
2 onions, sliced
2 garlic cloves, crushed
1 large red capsicum (pepper), cut into chunks
400 g (14 oz) zucchini (courgettes), cut into thick slices
400 g (14 oz) small waxy potatoes (such as Pontiac, kipfler or desiree), unpeeled, cut into 1 cm (1/2 inch) slices
1 kg (2 lb 4 oz) ripe tomatoes, peeled and roughly chopped
1 tsp dried oregano
2 tbs chopped flat-leaf (Italian) parsley
2 tbs chopped dill
1/2 tsp ground cinnamon

Heat 2 tablespoons of the olive oil in a heavy-based frying pan. Add the onion and cook over medium heat, stirring frequently until soft, about 10 minutes. Now add the garlic and cook for another 2 minutes.

Meanwhile, place all the other vegetables, herbs and spices in a large bowl and season well with salt and pepper. Add the softened onion mixture and toss everything together.

Transfer to a large baking dish and drizzle the remaining oil over the top. Cover and bake in a 180°C (350°F/Gas 4) oven for 1–1 1/2 hours, or until all the vegetables are tender, stirring every 30 minutes. Serve hot with crusty bread or rice.
Serves 4.

pumpkin and feta pie

700 g (1 lb 9 oz) butternut pumpkin (squash),
cut into 2 cm (3/4 inch) pieces
4 garlic cloves, unpeeled
4 tbs olive oil
2 small red onions, halved and sliced
1 tbs balsamic vinegar
1 tbs soft brown sugar
100 g (3 1/2 oz) good-quality feta cheese,
broken into small pieces
1 tbs chopped rosemary
1 large sheet ready-rolled shortcrust pastry

Put the pumpkin and garlic on a baking tray, drizzle with half the olive oil and bake in a 200°C (400°F/Gas 6) oven until the pumpkin is tender, about 25–30 minutes. Remove from the oven and leave to cool.

Meanwhile, caramelize the onions. Heat the rest of the oil in a small frying pan and cook the onion over medium heat for 10 minutes, giving it a good stir now and then. Add the vinegar and sugar and cook for another 15 minutes, or until the onion is nicely caramelized. Scoop the onion into a large bowl with the pumpkin and cool completely.

Add the feta and rosemary to the pumpkin mixture. Squeeze the garlic flesh out of its skin and mix it through the vegetables. Season with salt and ground pepper.

Roll out the pastry between two sheets of baking paper to a 35 cm (14 inch) circle. Remove the top sheet and place the bottom sheet with the pastry on a baking tray. Spoon the pumpkin mixture over the pastry, leaving a 4 cm (1 1/2 inch) border. Working your way around, fold over the edges of the pastry, pleating as you fold. Now bake your pie for 30 minutes, or until the pastry is crisp and golden. Great with a fresh green salad. Serves 6.

Eating humble pie has
never been so easy. Here
a gentle roasting makes the
humblest ingredients sublime.
A sprig of rosemary makes
them unforgettable.

on the side

little extras to put some
pizazz on your plate

This feisty salad gets its sweet, sharp kick from the sensual pomegranate, ubiquitous in the East yet mysteriously absent from Western cuisine. Look for large, darkly red fruits as they tend to be the sweetest and most succulent.

green olive, walnut and pomegranate salad

100 g (1 cup) walnut halves
350 g (12 oz) green olives, pitted
and cut in half
175 g (1 cup) pomegranate seeds
1 large red onion, chopped
20 g (1 cup) fresh flat-leaf (Italian) parsley

For the chilli pomegranate dressing:
125 ml (1/2 cup) olive oil
1 1/2 tbs pomegranate syrup
1/2 tsp chilli flakes

Soak the walnut halves in boiling water for 3–4 minutes, or until the skins peel off readily. Drain, peel and pat the walnuts dry, then lightly toast them under a medium grill (broiler). Let the walnuts cool, then roughly chop them and toss into a serving bowl.

Meanwhile, make the chilli pomegranate dressing. Simply put all the ingredients in a screw-top jar and shake well.

Throw the olives, pomegranate seeds, onion and parsley into the serving bowl and toss with the toasted walnuts. When you're ready to serve, drizzle the dressing over the salad, season to taste, and toss it all together one last time.
Serves 4.

green beans with tomato and olive oil

4 tbs olive oil
1 large onion, chopped
3 garlic cloves, finely chopped
400 g (14 oz) can good-quality
chopped tomatoes
1/2 tsp sugar
750 g (1 lb 10 oz) green beans, trimmed
3 tbs chopped fresh flat-leaf (Italian) parsley

Heat the olive oil in a large frying pan, add the onion and cook over medium heat for 5 minutes, or until softened. Add the garlic and cook for another 30 seconds.

Now add the tomatoes, sugar and 125 ml (1/2 cup) water, then season to taste. Bring to the boil, then reduce the heat and let the mixture simmer for 10 minutes, or until reduced slightly.

Stir in the beans and simmer for another 10 minutes, or until they are tender and the tomato mixture is pulpy. Stir in the parsley, check the seasoning, and serve up while lovely and hot.
Serves 4.

The aroma from a bubbling pot can have a whole street salivating, but for serious power on the plate, colour is the key. With its vibrant greens and resplendent reds, this dish looks every bit as fresh and fabulous as it tastes.

A striking dish with an alluring note of nutmeg, this tian is dressed to impress. Serve it when special guests are coming for dinner — just don't let on how easy it was!

vegetable tian

3 tbs olive oil
500 g (1 lb 2 oz) zucchini (courgettes),
thickly sliced on the diagonal
4 garlic cloves, crushed
pinch of freshly grated nutmeg
650 g (1 lb 7 oz) ripe tomatoes
2 red onions, chopped
3 tbs white wine
20 g (1 cup) chopped flat-leaf (Italian) parsley
125 g (4½ oz) Gruyère cheese, grated
a few small thyme sprigs

Heat half the oil in a large frying pan. Add the zucchini and half the garlic and cook, stirring now and then, over low heat until just beginning to soften, about 8 minutes. Stir in the nutmeg, season well with salt and pepper, then arrange the zucchini slices in the bottom of a greased 25 x 15 cm (10 x 6 inch) ovenproof dish.

Next, peel the tomatoes. The easiest way to do this is to score a cross in the base of each of them, then sit them in a bowl of boiling water for 10 seconds. Plunge into cold water and peel the skin away from the cross. Now roughly chop the tomatoes.

Now add the remaining oil to the frying pan and cook the onion over low heat for 5 minutes, stirring often. Add the remaining garlic along with the tomatoes, wine and parsley. Cook, stirring often, until all the liquid has evaporated, about 10 minutes.

Finally, assemble the tian. Sprinkle the cheese over the zucchini slices and spread the tomato mixture over the top. Scatter with thyme sprigs and bake in a 180°C (350°F/Gas 4) oven for 20 minutes, or until heated through. Cut into equal portions and lift out using a cake server or spatula. Serves 4.

gratin dauphinois

1 kg (2 lb 4 oz) floury potatoes, peeled
2 garlic cloves, crushed
70 g (2^1/$_2$ oz) Gruyère cheese, grated
pinch of freshly grated nutmeg
300 ml (10^1/$_2$ fl oz) thick (double/heavy) cream
100 ml (3^1/$_2$ fl oz) milk

Thinly slice the potatoes using a mandolin or sharp knife.

Arrange a layer of the potato slices in a buttered 23 x 16 cm (9 x 6^1/$_2$ inch) ovenproof dish. Sprinkle with a little garlic, grated cheese, nutmeg and seasoning. Add another layer of potato slices, then sprinkle with a little more garlic, grated cheese, nutmeg and seasoning. Repeat until you've used up all the potato slices, but save some of the cheese.

Now pour the cream and milk over the top and sprinkle with the remaining cheese.

Bake in a 170°C (325°F/Gas 3) oven until the potatoes are completely cooked and the liquid absorbed — this will take about 50–60 minutes. If the top starts to brown too much, cover loosely with foil. Leave to rest for 10 minutes before serving.
Serves 6.

Some nights, nothing will do but one of the classics — and right up there at the apex of home-spun classy comforts sits the gratin dauphinois.

Roasting draws out the sweetness of root vegetables, rendering them crisp and caramel on the outside, and creamy on the inside. Mustard and vinegar create a lovely acidic counterpoint.

roast winter vegetable salad

500 g (1 lb 2 oz) new potatoes, halved
6 parsnips, quartered lengthways
500 g (1 lb 2 oz) orange sweet potato,
peeled and cut into large pieces
400 g (14 oz) turnips, quartered
350 g (12 oz) baby carrots
4 baby onions, halved
olive oil, for drizzling

For the dressing:
125 ml (1/2 cup) orange juice
1 tbs Dijon mustard
1 tsp tarragon vinegar
1 tsp macadamia oil

Grab a large roasting tin and put all the vegetables in it, in a single layer. Drizzle them with some olive oil and toss to coat. Bake in a 200°C (400°F/Gas 6) oven until the vegetables are crisp and tender, about 50 minutes.

Meanwhile, make the dressing. Simply put all the ingredients in a bowl and whisk together well.

Scoop the roasted vegetables into a large salad bowl, drizzle with the dressing and gently toss to combine. This is a dish you could serve hot or cold.
Serves 6.

grilled vegetable salad

2 eggplants (aubergines), sliced diagonally
4 zucchini (courgettes), sliced diagonally
1 yellow capsicum (pepper), grilled (broiled),
peeled and cut into wide strips
1 red capsicum (pepper), grilled (broiled),
peeled and cut into wide strips

For the dressing:
2 garlic cloves
1 heaped tsp sea salt
150 ml (5 fl oz) extra virgin olive oil
juice of 1 small lemon or 3 tbs
red wine vinegar
1/2 red chilli, finely chopped
3 tbs torn basil
6 peppercorns, crushed

Firstly, a tip on chargrilling vegetables: don't brush the griddle or vegetables with oil, as the oil will burn and taste bitter. If the metal is hot enough, the vegetables won't stick. To give the vegetables a lovely crosshatched look, leave them undisturbed on the griddle until the first set of chargrill lines appear, then neatly rotate them 90 degrees to complete the crosshatched effect.

So let's get started. Heat a chargrill pan (griddle) or barbecue hotplate to very hot. Grill a few eggplant slices over medium–high heat, until golden and softened on both sides. Cook all the eggplant in this way, stacking the cooked slices on top of each other to steam and soften them a little more. Cook the zucchini in the same way until dark golden brown, and put them with the eggplant.

To make the dressing, smash the garlic with the sea salt in a mortar and pestle — or coat a knife blade in the salt and scrape it against the garlic in a downwards motion until it forms a paste. Now mix the crushed garlic together with the olive oil, lemon juice, chilli, basil and peppercorns.

Finally, arrange the vegetables in a flat dish and pour the dressing over. Mix gently and marinate for at least 30 minutes or overnight. Mix in the basil just before serving.
Serves 6.

This simple, summery salad showcases vegetables at their best. Cook them in advance and allow the bright, glistening capsicums and silky eggplants to soak up the deliciously garlicky dressing.

We say tomato, the Italians say pomodoro, and in days of old, people knew these succulent red fruits as love apples. Roasting teases out their tarty sweetness, releasing an explosion of liquid and flavour — love at first bite.

oven-roasted tomatoes

12 large ripe tomatoes, sliced in
half horizontally
150 ml (5 fl oz) extra virgin olive oil
3 garlic cloves, chopped
2 tbs finely chopped thyme or rosemary
30 g (1/2 cup) finely chopped parsley

Put the tomatoes on a lightly greased baking tray or in a very shallow gratin dish, and season with salt and pepper.

Slosh together the remaining ingredients, and drizzle 2 teaspoons of the mixture over the top of each tomato. Bake for 2–3 hours in a 180°C (350°F/Gas 4) oven — the tomatoes should be caramelized and crisp on top and quite shrivelled, with all the liquid having reduced inside them.

If the tomatoes are cooking too quickly and are starting to become too brown or burn, turn the heat down. If a pool of oil collects around the tomatoes, use it to baste the roasting tomatoes to keep the tops moist. These tomatoes are equally delicious served hot or cold.
Serves 6.

braised fennel with olives

2 large fennel bulbs
4 tbs extra virgin olive oil
1 red onion, halved and thinly sliced
3 garlic cloves, sliced
4 small sprigs of rosemary, chopped
100 ml (3½ fl oz) white wine
50 g (1¾ oz) black olives, pitted and halved

Slice the fennel into thick wedges, cutting from top to bottom but keeping them joined at the root. Cut off and reserve any fronds. Heat the olive oil in a large frying pan and cook the fennel and onion over medium heat until lightly browned, about 10 minutes, stirring every so often.

Now add the garlic and half the rosemary, season with salt and pepper and stir briefly to stop the fennel and garlic burning. After a few minutes, splash in the wine, pop the lid on and gently cook for another 10–15 minutes, or until the fennel is tender but still holding together. Check now and then to make sure it isn't burning. Just before the end of cooking, stir in the olives and the rest of the chopped rosemary.

Once the fennel is soft, it is cooked — it should be moist but not dry. If all the liquid has evaporated and the fennel still isn't cooked, add a splash more wine or water. If the fennel is almost cooked and there is a lot of liquid left, take the lid off to let the liquid reduce a little. Serve sprinkled with the reserved fronds.
Serves 4.

Mild, sweet and aromatic, fennel loves to be braised and served meltingly soft. A scattering of olives adds a sharp, salty twist.

Popeye popped spinach by the can, but here's a far more palatable way to pop a dose of iron!

sautéed spinach

1 kg (2 lb 4 oz) English spinach
2 tbs olive oil
1 garlic clove

Wash the spinach thoroughly and shake it dry, leaving just a little water clinging to the leaves.

Heat the oil in a frying pan and add the garlic. Cook for a few seconds over medium heat, then throw in the spinach. Cover the pan for a minute to create some steam.

Now remove the lid and turn up the heat, stirring the spinach until all the liquid has evaporated. Season and serve hot.
Serves 4.

marinated zucchini

500 g (1 lb 2 oz) small zucchini (courgettes),
thinly sliced on the diagonal
1 tbs olive oil
1 tbs finely chopped parsley
1 garlic clove, sliced
1 tbs balsamic or red wine vinegar

Heat the oil in a heavy-based frying pan and fry the zucchini slices in batches over medium heat until nicely browned all over — about 1 minute each side. Remove with a slotted spoon, drain, and place in a non-metallic dish.

Make a simple marinade by swishing all the remaining ingredients about in a screw-top jar. Pour it over the zucchini, season well, and leave for a few hours to let the flavours soak in. Delicious on an antipasto platter. Serves 4.

Whether you call them zucchini or courgettes, make sure you select small, sweet baby ones for this garlicky, vinegary, delectable dish.

Divinely light and fluffy and ever so tasty, this version of mash is far from the lumpy sludge of childhood memories. Mash up an enormous vat of it — the only cries you're going to hear are more, more, more!

mashed potato

1 kg (2 lb 4 oz) floury potatoes, peeled
250 ml (1 cup) milk
4 tbs extra virgin olive oil
75 g (3/4 cup) grated Parmesan cheese
freshly grated nutmeg

Cut the potatoes into large, even pieces and cook them in boiling salted water until tender, about 12 minutes. Carefully scoop them into a colander and drain well.

Now pour the milk into the saucepan and heat it briefly, then add the potatoes and mash well until very smooth.

Beat in the olive oil and Parmesan and season with salt, pepper and the nutmeg. Serve piping hot without delay.
Serves 4.

tabbouleh with soy grits

150 g (1 bunch) flat-leaf (Italian) parsley
180 g (1 cup) soy grits
2 tbs chopped mint
1 small red onion, cut into thin wedges
3 ripe tomatoes, chopped
400 g (14 oz) can chickpeas, rinsed and drained
3 tbs lemon juice
2 tbs extra virgin olive oil
Lebanese, Turkish or pitta bread

Firstly, remove all the stalks from the parsley. Roughly chop the leaves and toss them into a large serving bowl.

Put the soy grits in a heatproof bowl and pour in 170 ml ($2/3$ cup) boiling water. Leave to soak for 3 minutes, or until all the water has been absorbed.

Now add the soy grits to the parsley, along with the mint, onion, tomato and chickpeas. Drizzle with the lemon juice and olive oil, season well with salt and freshly ground black pepper, then toss it all together. Terrific with Lebanese, Turkish or pitta bread spread with a good dollop of hummus. Serves 6–8.

Intensely herby, a mouthful of tabbouleh is an invigorating experience. It's almost too good to be relegated to the side — you could happily eat a big bowl of it with fresh Turkish bread for lunch!

The marriage of aniseed and orange is one made in heaven. Roasting the fennel softens the flavour and gives it depth, providing a perfect springboard for a citrus splash.

roasted fennel and orange salad

8 baby fennel bulbs
125 ml (1/2 cup) olive oil
2 oranges
1 red onion, halved and thinly sliced
100 g (3 1/2 oz) Kalamata olives
1 tbs lemon juice
2 tbs roughly chopped mint
1 tbs chopped flat-leaf (Italian) parsley

Trim the fronds off the fennel and reserve. Remove the stalks and cut a 5 mm (1/4 inch) thick slice off the base of each fennel bulb. Slice each bulb into 6 wedges, place in a roasting tin and drizzle with 1/3 cup (about 4 tablespoons) of the olive oil. Season well. Bake in a 200°C (400°F/Gas 6) oven until tender and slightly caramelized, about 40–45 minutes, turning once or twice during cooking. Allow to cool.

Meanwhile, cut a thin slice off the top and bottom of each orange. Using a small sharp knife, slice the skin and pith off, removing as much pith as possible. Now remove the membranes from all the orange segments. To do this, slice down the side of a segment between the flesh and the membrane. Repeat on the other side and lift the segment out — do this over a bowl to catch all the orange juice. Repeat with all the segments, and squeeze out any juice left in the membranes. Throw the orange segments into a serving dish with the onion and olives.

Whisk the remaining oil into the orange juice and lemon juice until emulsified. Season well. Pour half the dressing over the oranges with half the mint. Mix well. Add the fennel, drizzle with the rest of the dressing, and scatter with the remaining herbs. Sprinkle with the reserved fennel fronds and serve. Serves 4.

panzanella

900 g (2 lb) ripe tomatoes, peeled
and quartered
3 garlic cloves, crushed
30 g (1 cup) basil, torn, plus a few
whole leaves
4 tbs red wine vinegar
300 ml (10 1/2 fl oz) extra virgin olive oil
1 day-old 'country-style' loaf (such as
ciabatta), crust removed, cut into
4 cm (1 1/2 inch) cubes
1 small cucumber, peeled and deseeded
2 red capsicums (peppers), peeled
and cut into thick strips
2 yellow capsicums (peppers), peeled
and cut into thick strips
50 g (1 3/4 oz) capers, rinsed and squeezed dry
100 g (3 1/2 oz) black olives, pitted and halved

Hold each tomato quarter over a large bowl and squeeze the seeds and juice out into the bowl. Add the garlic, half the basil, the vinegar and 200 ml (7 fl oz) of the olive oil. Taste for seasoning.

Toss in the bread and the tomato quarters, then leave for at least 30 minutes. If the bread is quite hard, it may need more liquid — if so, add more olive oil and vinegar in equal proportions.

Thinly slice the cucumber and add to the bowl, then divide half the mixture among six plates. Top with half the capsicum, then sprinkle with half the capers, half the olives and the remaining basil. Spoon the last of the bread mixture over the top and sprinkle with the remaining capsicum, capers and olives. The salad can be left for up to 2 hours, but serve it at room temperature, not straight from the fridge.

Just before serving, scatter with basil leaves and drizzle with the remaining olive oil. Serves 6.

If you just can't finish a meal without wiping the plate clean, this is the dish for you. Traditionally a thrifty way of using up leftover bread, now just pleasure on a plate.

Vivid colours, intense flavours and an interplay of textures make an impressive meal of this spectacular salad.

fresh beetroot and goat's cheese salad

1 kg (2 lb 4 oz) fresh beetroot
(4 bulbs with leaves)
200 g (7 oz) green beans, trimmed
100 g (3 1/2 oz) goat's cheese, crumbled

For the caper dressing:
1 tbs red wine vinegar
2 tbs extra virgin olive oil
1 garlic clove, crushed
1 tbs capers, rinsed, squeezed dry and
coarsely chopped

Trim the leaves from the beetroot. Scrub the bulbs and wash the leaves well. Put the bulbs in a large saucepan of salted water. Bring to the boil, then reduce the heat, pop a lid on and simmer until tender, about 30 minutes. Drain the beetroots and let them cool a little.

Meanwhile, bring another saucepan of water to the boil. Add the beans and cook until just tender, about 3 minutes. Remove with a slotted spoon, plunge into a bowl of cold water and drain well. Now add the beetroot leaves to the same pan of water and cook until tender, about 3–5 minutes. Remove the leaves, plunge into a bowl of cold water, then drain them well.

Back to those beetroot bulbs. Slip on a pair of kitchen gloves and peel the skins off, then cut the bulbs into thin wedges.

Finally, put all the caper dressing ingredients in a screw-top jar with 1/2 teaspoon each of salt and pepper. Give it a good shake.

Time to eat! Divide the beans, beetroot leaves and beetroot wedges among four serving plates. Sprinkle with goat's cheese and drizzle with the caper dressing. Delicious served with fresh crusty bread. Serves 4.

gorgeous greek salad

1 telegraph cucumber, peeled
2 green capsicums (peppers), cut into
1 cm ($^1/_2$ inch) chunks
4 vine-ripened tomatoes, sliced into wedges
1 red onion, thinly sliced
16 Kalamata olives
250 g (9 oz) Greek feta cheese, cubed
24 flat-leaf (Italian) parsley leaves
12 whole mint leaves

For the dressing:
125 ml ($^1/_2$ cup) extra virgin olive oil
2 tbs lemon juice
1 garlic clove, crushed

This salad is stupendously simple. Cut the cucumber in half lengthways and discard the seeds. Cut into bite-sized pieces and toss into a large salad bowl, then add the remaining salad ingredients and gently toss together.

Put the dressing ingredients in a screw-top jar, season well and give it a hearty shake. Pour over the salad and serve.
Serves 6.

Transport yourself to a cliff-top terrace in Santorini with every salty, crispy, refreshing bite of this celebrated salad. It draws upon the simplest of ingredients, so quality is paramount — only the freshest vegetables and finest fixings will do.

Swelling from a tiny grain into a satisfying salad in a matter of minutes, couscous is the ultimate fast food. For a Middle Eastern medley, toss in a handful each of sultanas, shredded dried apricots and dates, pine nuts, coriander and lemon zest.

couscous salad

100 g (3¹/2 oz) green beans, trimmed and halved
300 g (10¹/2 oz) orange sweet potato, peeled and cubed
350 g (12 oz) instant couscous
500 ml (2 cups) vegetable stock
200 g (7 oz) cherry tomatoes, halved
150 g (1 cup) frozen corn kernels, thawed
155 g (1 cup) frozen peas, thawed
1 red capsicum (pepper), chopped
60 g (1 cup) chopped parsley
25 g (¹/2 cup) chopped mint

For the dressing:
2 garlic cloves, crushed
3 tbs lemon juice
1 tbs oil
1 tbs white wine vinegar
1 tsp Dijon mustard
1 tsp honey

Bring a saucepan of water to the boil. Add the beans and cook until just tender, about 3 minutes. Remove the beans with a slotted spoon, plunge into a bowl of cold water and drain well.

Now add the sweet potato to the same saucepan of water and cook until tender, about 8 minutes. Drain well.

Meanwhile, heat the stock in a small saucepan. Place the couscous in a large bowl and pour on the hot stock. Pop a lid on and let the couscous sit for 5 minutes, or until all the stock has been absorbed. Fluff up the grains with a fork, then toss in the beans, sweet potato, cherry tomatoes, corn, peas, capsicum and herbs. Mix well.

For the finishing touch, whisk all the dressing ingredients together in a bowl. Pour the dressing over the couscous salad and toss together well.
Serves 4.

index